A Guide to Nonprofit Board Success

A Guide to Nonprofit Board Success

Answering the Call of Leadership

Cynthia Jarboe

Foreword by Timothy J. Sullivan

 PRAEGER®

An Imprint of ABC-CLIO, LLC

Santa Barbara, California • Denver, Colorado

Library of Congress Cataloging in Publication Control Number: 2019025710

ISBN: 978-1-4408-7266-2 (print)
 978-1-4408-7267-9 (ebook)

24 23 22 21 20   1 2 3 4 5

This book is also available as an eBook.

Praeger
An Imprint of ABC-CLIO, LLC

ABC-CLIO, LLC
147 Castilian Drive
Santa Barbara, California 93117
www.abc-clio.com

This book is printed on acid-free paper ∞

Manufactured in the United States of America

Contents

Foreword

This is a book well worth reading. When I reviewed the manuscript, its quality did not surprise. During my time as president of William & Mary, Cindy Jarboe and I worked together closely. She was one of the college's ablest volunteer leaders. She never failed. She was conscientious, imaginative, and indefatigable. The intensity of her commitment inspired others.

This book deserves a wide audience for many reasons. Among them is the underappreciated importance of nonprofit organizations. Consider this: in one recent year the nonprofit sector contributed $878 billion to the national economy. That approximates 5.5% of our gross domestic product. Nearly 12 million people find employment in the nonprofit sector, more than 10% of the American workforce.

Nonprofits are not principally engines of economic growth. They touch every aspect of the cultural, educational, and moral life of the nation. Choose any American city or town. You will discover profound nonprofit influence everywhere: in the arts, education, the environment, health, and religion. Put simply, life without nonprofits is unimaginable.

What also makes this book special is the wide-angle analytic lens Cindy uses in shaping its content. Here the reader will discover informed advice on every aspect of nonprofit endeavors, from the essentials of volunteer recruitment to the basis of financial literacy and to the ABCs of event planning. Nothing important has been omitted.

Yet this book is much more than a well-considered "how to" manual. Cindy writes with real insight about leadership. She is a wise guide to what makes great leaders and how they may be trained and sustained. Her thinking is relevant to leaders and leadership in any context.

If the lessons this book tries to teach are taken to heart, the wide world of nonprofits will be better managed and led. This, in turn, will make nonprofits everywhere more effective servants of the great causes in aid of which they were founded.

Timothy J. Sullivan

Timothy J. Sullivan was the 25th president of the College of William & Mary from 1992 through 2005. After receiving his law degree from Harvard University, he was professor at the Marshall-Wythe School of Law where he became dean in 1985. He served for nearly three years as executive assistant for policy for then Virginia governor Charles S. Robb. He served as president and chief executive officer of The Mariner's Museum from 2006 through 2009. He is active with numerous nonprofits and has been appointed to numerous commissions, task forces, and the Council of Presidents where he was chair of the governing board.

Preface

These days, it is busy people who step forward and agree to serve on nonprofit boards. Often when they join their first board or even subsequent boards, they do not know what they are getting themselves into. They do not have the time to read textbooks or the latest in-depth thinking on governance of nonprofits. They need a quick, easy read on the basics of what it means to join the board of a nonprofit. Additionally, officers of boards do not have the time to teach all the principles that they may have learned from decades of board service. Often board terms are limited to three to six years, and there are always new board members coming on. This book of basic principles can be read in a few hours but serve as a refresher and a reference for board members. Resources such as sample policies, forms, and checklists are provided for future reference.

Given the often-limited number of board meetings held and the amount of business that needs to be addressed, training is often nonexistent or limited to a couple of hours. New board members have to get up to speed quickly. This book answers many of the "I wish I had known that when I first went on the board" questions.

As the numbers of nonprofits continue to grow with the emphasis on social responsibility, the need for knowledgeable board members grows. This book, based on over 35 years of both serving on boards and providing financial and consulting services to boards and nonprofit organizations, is intended to meet the need to provide a basic understanding of what board members will have to understand to participate effectively.

At the same time, fraudulent and irresponsible nonprofits also continue to grow increasing the need for transparency; fiscal responsibility; and skilled, ethical board members. With the availability of data on nonprofits on the Internet, board members need to know how to represent their organizations well from day one in any setting. This book meets that need by discussing how information about a nonprofit organization is derived for publication on the Internet and the board's responsibility for accuracy and favorable portrayal.

Having consulted with and served on almost 100 nonprofit boards in my 36-year career, I have been asked often if there is an easy-to-read resource to help new board members get up to speed quickly. The topics covered in this book are the essential topics that apply to almost all boards. The organization of the book parallels a new board member's experience from the first invitation to be nominated to the board, the first meeting, and then the topics the board member will have to address. Each chapter is organized with a light introduction sharing the current experience of the novice board member, a discussion of the concepts, and finally a section called "Reality Check," which is a miniature case study or anecdote that reiterates many of the topics covered in the chapter.

This book is intended to easily assist new board members in understanding their roles and responsibilities starting with the decision on whether to join a board. It then covers what to expect in the first board meeting, including how a board member should prepare followed by board governance, including committee service and the relationship between the board and staff. Other topics covered are fund-raising, how to read nonprofit financial statements, understand investing, and the endowment model and the importance of strategic planning. Additional topics include event planning, technology, evaluation of boards and their members, and recruiting volunteers. After all the technical and best practices are covered, the final chapter addresses leadership skills and what history has shown the traits of good leaders are.

This book was written for prospective, new, and experienced board members, each of whom can use this book as a handy checklist for basic best practices for board leadership. Key committee members and staff would benefit from the book. Often volunteers serve on key committees as training for possible future board positions and committee meetings should be run in a similar manner to board meetings.

On completion of this book, I hope you will feel confident to lead your organization toward its vison and mission.

A Personal Reality Check . . .

To my daughters, I hope that you have the opportunity to experience the treasures I have gained through serving nonprofit organizations. The two of you are the treasures I am most proud of. Thank you for being on this journey with me.

CHAPTER ONE

Should I Serve?

Wow, I haven't heard from him in a long time! It was great catching up with my former college friend after 10 years. It took 20 minutes before he got to the real reason for his call. He wanted to know if I would consider serving on the Board of Trustees for the Iris Foundation. Apparently he's been on it for a few years and likes serving. I'm not sure exactly what they do, but he says it's a great honor to be asked and hardly means any time commitment. They just meet in person a few times a year, join in a few conference calls, and then the black-tie dinner event. I told him I would discuss it with my wife and get back to him. He said spouses all attend the dinner event, and his wife loves it. Wonder why I was asked? I did just make partner at my firm, and my wife is the daughter of the regional grocery store chain owner.

So you are flattered to be asked, he was a fun guy to hang around with in college, and you just know this board must have some amazing parties or he wouldn't be involved. But what questions do you or any potential board nominee need to ask?

1. Find out more about the organization. What is its purpose? Who started it, and when?

   • Key considerations

     • Never agree to serve an organization if you are not or do not think you can be passionate about its cause. You are going to represent the organization to the outside world, volunteer a lot of time, and make substantial financial donations to them. You want to put your heart and soul into this organization. You want to become vested in its purpose. You are also committing the support of your family to this organization since it will take time away from them and they will be asked to participate in the activities of the organization. Make sure they, too, can get excited about the group and want to participate.

- There are thousands of organizations you could get involved with and who need you. Pick the one or ones that you can both give and get the most from.

- When, by whom, and why the organization was started are all important in determining the level of effort that will be required of you. Serving the board of a start-up organization will take much more effort than an established one.

- Is the "founder" still involved? If so, is the organization still "controlled" by that one person? Are you in agreement with the direction the original founder is taking the organization? Will you have the opportunity to make a difference on the board, or are there one or a few individuals who still control the board and really are just trying to "fill the seats"?

2. Look into the financial situation of the organization. Do they have an endowment or other long-term investment fund or funds? Or are they on the brink of a financial disaster?

- Key considerations

  - What is their source of funding? Is it primarily government or private foundation grants? You may have read about organizations that have just had their funding cut substantially by a federal, state, or local government that had been providing the majority of their funding. That funding will have to be replaced, either by private donors or by significant program and administrative cost reductions. How much of their revenue is from individual donors or membership dues? The sources of funding change the dynamics and role of the board.

  - We will discuss what is meant by "endowment" in Chapter 6, but what you need to find out now is the financial focus for the organization. Is it a long-term focus from a financial perspective, meaning it has reserves, its invests funds raised, and it maintains those investments to ensure the future of the organization in perpetuity? Or does the organization live day to day, year to year, relying on this year's grants and donations to cover this year's expenses and program needs.

  - If the organization is surviving day to day or month to month, the focus will have to be on generating funds and probably not on the program needs of the organization.

- Perhaps the organization has a plan or strategy for a campaign that will ensure its future. We will discuss campaigns in Chapter 4, but understanding the board's strategy for dealing with the financial situation is important.

3. Who else serves on the board? Can you speak with another member you may know?

- Key considerations

  - Look at who else serves on the board. Are they community leaders with outstanding reputations, particularly for getting things done? Will you enjoy getting to know them better?

  - Contact one of them (besides your college friend), and ask about the person's involvement and time commitment. Ask open-ended questions such as how things are going with the organization.

  - Is the board made up of a diverse group of people? Every board needs representation from all demographics, employment backgrounds, ages, and races. Ideally, if it is an organization that serves a particular population, the board should include those with direct experience with that population, for example, if it is an educational organization, the parent of a student.

  - Does the board contain a good mix of those "lending their name and/or the support of their organization" (e.g., the mayor or chairman of the local bank) and "worker bees," those who are so committed to the cause they are willing and able to put in whatever time it takes to get the job done.

4. Is there a paid staff, or are the volunteers expected to carry out the administration and charitable purpose of the organization? How large and active is the volunteer network?

- Key considerations

  - Understanding the availability and roles of the staff helps quantify the expectations of the board and the volunteer network.

  - Most, if not all, well-run charitable organizations never have the number of staff they need to get the job done and, instead, rely on a network of volunteers. Ask how volunteers are recruited and how the number of volunteers is trending.

  - Who runs the major events? Are board committees supported by staff, or are the board and/or volunteers responsible for administrative activities? Time commitments for board members vary significantly based on the answer to these questions.

- How is the staff organized, what is their background, what is the rate of staff turnover, why do they leave? Does everyone understand their role? Is there a person responsible for development and finance, or is it outsourced and, if so, to whom? Hopefully not to a board member.

5. How does Charity Navigator or the Better Business Bureau rate the organization? Why does the organization have such a low or high rating?

- Key considerations

  - Several websites rate charitable organizations based typically on their tax filings that are available to the public and on complaints received.

  - One of the best known is Charity Navigator, which can be found at www.charitynavigator.org. It provides a numerical rating that may be dated, since it uses data from the last IRS (Internal Revenue Service) Form 990 filing, which is usually at least a year old. It rates organizations based on how much they spend on fund-raising and administration compared to their spending on programs and services. Charity Navigator frequently provides information on how much an organization is spending to raise a dollar. According to its site, it has over 1.6 million IRS-registered sites included. Charity Navigator rates charities on their financial health and their accountability and transparency, giving up to four stars for an overall rating based on the distance of the two ratings from a perfect score. When available, it provides a summary income statement, the purported mission, the compensation of the executive director, and trend information.

  - The second website worth reviewing is the Better Business Bureau site at www.bbb.org/charity-reviews/national. This site lists far fewer organizations, but for those listed, it indicates whether the organization meets the standards for charity accountability in the areas of governance, measuring effectiveness, and finances and fund-raising. It provides the purpose, programs, governance, and staff, including the compensation of the chief executive, tax status, and summary financial information. The summary financial information includes the percentages spent on programs versus fund-raising versus administration.

  - These sites are just starting points for information and may lead to a false conclusion or concerns. Generally, they provide information only for the most recent year available. For example, if an organization is currently conducting a major capital campaign, its fund-raising percentage and administrative expenses may be unusually high compared to other charities, thus lowering their rating.

6. Are they current on their tax and other filings?

    • Key considerations

        • All not-for-profit organizations are required to register as an exempt organization with the IRS and receive a tax determination letter stating that they qualify as an exempt organization. They should also obtain an employer identification number.

        • Annually, they are required to file an IRS Form 990 or one of the simpler variations, depending on their receipts for the year. At a minimum, every organization must file an electronic postcard listing its current mailing address, providing contact information, and verifying that it does not meet the requirements to file one of the other 990 forms.

        • Additionally, if they have unrelated business income as defined by the tax code, additional filings and the payment of taxes may be required.

        • States also require registration on an annual basis for the state they are headquartered in and for any state that they conduct certain activities in, such as fund-raising.

        • Before agreeing to serve, ask the staff or the accountant about the filing status of the tax returns and the related state annual reports and registrations.

7. Is the organization audited or reviewed, and by what firm or person? What is the frequency of the audits or reviews? Did it receive an unqualified opinion?

    • Key considerations

        • Every organization conducting fund-raising and/or holding investments should be either audited or reviewed by a certified public accountant, with the preference being an audit since that provides a higher level of comfort.

        • Some organizations alternate reviews and audits each year but often find that is just as expensive in the long run.

        • If they are audited, ask if they received an unmodified opinion since that indicates that—based on an audit conducted in accordance with the standards of the appropriate standard setting bodies—the financial statements are materially accurate and include all the required disclosures in accordance with generally accepted accounting principles.

8. Discuss the time commitments in detail. When and where are the meetings, conference calls, and events? Are board members reimbursed for their travel expenses? How many committees will you be asked to serve on, and when and how do they meet?

- Key considerations
    - Being a responsible board member means giving of your time based on the needs of the organization. You will not be an effective board member if you agree to serve and then get busy with work and are unable to contribute.
    - There are times when one's own career takes priority or family commitments become all-consuming. These are not the times to agree to serve. Ask for a deferral, or volunteer on a committee or a project that requires less time.
    - The worst thing a person recruiting a board member can do is minimize the time commitment to a prospective board member. Both will become frustrated.
    - Assess the financial expectations of board membership ahead of time. The financial expectations include cash donations, event ticket purchases, and self-funding of attendance at meetings and events. If you join the board of a major firm or corporation, it may pay for some or all.
    - If you are at a stage where it may not be possible to meet the personal financial commitments of serving, you can either make that clear to the person recruiting you or decline to serve. It is best to address the point up front rather than face embarrassment later.

9. What will your employer think about your involvement? Will your employer give you the time off to attend meetings, and will your employer match your contributions?

- Key considerations
    - Often employers encourage their employees to be active in the community, so speak with your employer about your opportunity to serve on the board.
    - Explain the time commitment, and ask that any time required during the workweek not be taken as vacation time since you are furthering the image of your employer through your involvement.
    - Large companies often have matching gift programs, and if you are lucky enough to work for one of those, your personal financial obligation has just been cut in half since your employer will pick up the other half.

10. Is there directors and officers insurance on board members?

- Key considerations
    - While lawsuits against nonprofit organizations may be less frequent than in the for-profit world, they do still occur. Therefore,

every nonprofit should include directors and officers insurance that will protect board members in the event of a lawsuit.

- If you rent a car for conducting business for the organization, always list your own name as well as the name of the organization so that the organization's auto insurance will cover you in the event of an accident.

11. How long is my term, or is it a life-time appointment?

- Key considerations

  - How long are you willing to serve? Ask about the length of the terms and opportunities for reelection or appointment if there are term limits.

  - If you are being asked to fill the unexpired term of another board member, your term will end when that board member's term was scheduled to end.

  - Terms and term limits are normally spelled out in the bylaws of the organization but may be found in the articles of incorporation if the organization has them.

  - If you serve as an officer, there may be a provision to extend a term. For example, if you serve as board president, there may be a provision to extend your service by a year as the immediate past president in order to provide continuity for your successor.

12. Why do you think you would be a good fit for this particular board? Do you have a particular skill set or expertise needed on the board?

- Key considerations

  - If the nominating committee is doing their job, you were suggested because they had a need for a particular skill set or expertise.

  - For example, if your professional background is in finance or accounting, they may need your expertise in those areas. That means you will likely be asked to serve on the finance and investments committee(s) and perhaps be put in line for treasurer.

  - It may be that you were asked to serve because you represent a particular demographic or they want to develop a relationship with your employer or family. All of that is good governance as long as you are comfortable with that and are willing to assume responsibility for that representation.

13. What is the expected financial commitment of board members? Is it a multiyear pledge? Since you are expected to attend the events such as the black-tie gala, how much are the tickets for that, and are board members expected to fill a table?

- Key considerations

  - The old saying is that every board member should give their time, talent, and treasure. Some boards set a minimum cash contribution expectation. Some just expect every board member to give something as they are capable.

  - Find out the expectations and whether the contribution can be pledged and then paid over a few years or whether it is an annual commitment.

  - Also, figure in the cost of attending the events, which can be major fund-raising efforts and quite expensive.

  - As mentioned earlier, there may be an opportunity for your employer to share in this obligation. Sometimes the commitment is to raise a certain dollar amount, meaning you get credit for sponsorships or other contributions you bring in.

14. Are any capital campaigns in process and expected during your term? What are the expectations for board members related to the campaign?

  - Key considerations

    - A capital campaign is a multiyear fund-raising campaign normally designed to raise significant funds (millions or even billions) for specified major needs such as building projects or endowments to ensure the functioning of the organization in perpetuity.

    - While these campaigns may and should have their own steering committees, board participation is critical in both gifts and time. After all, it is difficult to ask for major gifts if the board members are not stepping forward with their own major gifts. Board members are often asked to participate in asking for major gifts, hosting events, and providing information on potential major gift donors.

    - Capital campaigns are in addition to the annual contributions that organizations rely on to continue their daily operations and programs and typically involve a multiyear pledge.

    - Some campaigns have a deferred giving component, meaning including the organization in your estate provisions.

15. Are there any potential conflicts of interest related to serving on the board?

  - Key considerations

    - Best practices for nonprofit organizations include having each board member sign a statement that they or their immediate family have no relationship with the organization that represents a conflict of interest.

- Conflicts of interest occur whenever you or your immediate family would benefit financially from an action taken by the board or the organization. Conflict of interest statements are discussed further in Chapter 2.

- In addition, a conflict of interest can occur if the organization grants funding to an organization that you or a member of your immediate family serves as a member of the board or as a staff member or significantly benefits from.

- If you are an officer of a company that has a significant contract to provide services or goods to the organization, that would represent a conflict, and you should not serve as a board member.

- The board's conflict of interest policy, which is discussed in Chapter 2, defines what a conflict of interest is and whom it relates to. When in doubt, ask.

16. Meet with the executive director and ask how the staff and board work together.

   - Key considerations

      - Does the board have a strategic plan and confine itself to strategic issues?

      - Try to get a sense as to whether the board is involved in day-to-day operating activities.

      - Ask the executive director for their expectations of a board member and what skill sets are currently needed on the board.

      - Ask the executive director what keeps them awake at night. What are the challenges the organization is facing?

      - Have the executive director introduce you to a few key staff and observe how they interact with each other.

Each of these questions will help you understand the organization, its culture, and how you might fit. You are trying to get a sense of the quality of the organization and the board. Your friend may be trying to sell you on the fun he is having, but serving on a board is hard work and there are legal and ethical responsibilities. You need to have a clear understanding of what you are getting yourself into.

Ask yourself after completing your inquiries why you want to be a leader of this organization. It might be because it is a vibrant, growing organization and you want to be part of the "winning team." It might be because the organization helped you or your family in the past, and you want to pay it back. It may be because you have a long-term relationship with the organization having been a member for a long time. Now you want to improve your leadership skills by serving in a more important role. It might be because you know the organization needs you and you will gain incredible satisfaction from getting it to the next level or even prevent it from dissolving. All great reasons to join the board.

If they are having significant problems or their future financial sustainability is in question, additional due diligence may be in order. Speak with multiple board members, stakeholders, and staff asking about the obstacles to their success. Are these obstacles that can be overcome? Are the board and staff willing to work together, listening to advice in order to address issues? Are there personnel issues that need to be addressed? Are there board personality or behavioral style issues that are causing problems?

Has anyone questioned the integrity or fiscal responsibility of those involved with the organization? Unfortunately, there have been plenty of examples where executive directors took large compensation packages or their travel expenses were lavish. While a prospective board member can't ask for details on compensation packages, they can get a sense of the control environment that would prevent such a situation. The IRS Form 990 now has questions and disclosures about such matters. Another indication that you may want to walk away is if there has been excessive board turnover from resignations. Resignations occur due to personal reasons but normally do not involve several board members leaving at the same time. If you know one of the board members who left, contact the person to ask for the reasons for leaving. Ask the person what they enjoyed most and liked least about serving on the board.

There are so many nonprofit organizations that could benefit from your experience. Do not waste your valuable time and funds if you will not be respected or the issues facing the organization are insurmountable. This chapter cannot end on this negative note because there are many nonprofit success stories that you are going to want to be part of.

Once you determine that this is an organization that deserves your time, talent, and treasure, you need to ask yourself if this is the time in your life to say "yes." As mentioned earlier, discuss the commitment with your family since they will be part of the organization as well. You may think you are letting the organization down by saying "no" because you do not have the time right now. The opposite is true. Saying "yes" and then not being able to devote the time and resources to the organization hurts the nonprofit far more. You are taking a seat that could be occupied by someone who can be fully committed. There will be a better time for you to serve as a leader of the organization.

At some point it will be the right time and right organization for your leadership, and you decide you would like to serve on the board. Determine the process for nomination to the board. Does the governance or nominating committee present multiple candidates for each board position, or is it a slate where the number of nominees equals the openings? If there are multiple candidates for each slot, what are the guidelines for election? Are you expected or permitted to "campaign"? Too often, such situations result in disappointment and the loss of great leaders, volunteers, and donors. The best practice to avoid such situations is for a strong governance committee to nominate one person for each opening.

Let's fast-forward and offer congratulations to your election to the board. Now the learning, fun, and friendships begin. Enjoy the experience!

Reality Check

The aforementioned points are some of the best practices a potential board member should consider. However, at the end of the day, your gut should tell you whether this is something you want to do. Let me tell you about my experience in deciding to join a board and the ultimate impact on my life.

Thirty years ago, a memo circulated around my public accounting firm to the effect that the Virginia Special Olympics was looking for a board member with financial expertise. I had just been promoted to manager, I had just had my first child, and my husband traveled a great deal with his job. I think I had been through three childcare providers in three months. The last thing I had time for was serving on the board of an organization I knew very little about. Therefore, I just passed the memo on to my counterparts. A week later, the same memo came around again, this time with a note from the managing partner that he really felt this was a worthy cause and wanted one of us to step forward. I looked into it further and saw that they had a large volunteer base and a full staff, but there was no one on the board I knew, and they met at various locations around the state, usually in conjunction with events/competitions. While I knew little about the mentally handicapped, the pictures and smiles on the website won me over, and I agreed to serve.

Somehow I found time to hire a new finance staff member, find an auditing firm, attend all the meetings and regional and state games, and serve as treasurer. It was one of the best experiences of my life. Not only did I gain leadership, strategic planning, and marketing skills that certainly aided in making partner with my firm, but I made lifelong friends and gained an appreciation for those with intellectual and physical disabilities and their families. The tears I shed as I watched how important this organization was to these very special athletes and their families, and the love they shared with me, were worth so much more than every minute of my time. I met incredible national leaders, including the founder of Special Olympics, Inc., Eunice Kennedy Shriver. My three-year-old daughter and I traveled cross-country with another board member and her Special Olympian son to the first International Special Olympics and got to attend the opening ceremonies with its celebrity cast. Even at her young age, she gained such an understanding and appreciation for those who were different from herself. I have to add it was that Special Olympian who pulled my daughter out at the motel pool when she got in over her head while his mother and I were chatting away on the side.

Later I was able to help host a delegation from the former USSR as they evaluated whether to start a Special Olympics-type program. This was a major step forward for them since their normal practice was to institutionalize those with intellectual disabilities. At the Second International Special Olympic games, my entire family traveled to Minnesota and helped present awards (alongside an actor for the *M*A*S*H* television series, I might add). My leadership presentation skills were further developed by conducting a workshop at the National Leadership Conference for Special Olympics. As you can tell, I got so much more than I gave by saying "yes" to serve on the board of the Virginia Special Olympics when my mind had originally said "no."

CHAPTER TWO

The Board Meeting or How Not to Feel Overwhelmed

Congratulations! You have been elected to the board of directors of the College of Ivy Foundation. You are eagerly looking forward to your first meeting next week, with committee meetings the afternoon of the first day, an awards dinner that night, and the board meeting the next day. You have received an e-mail letting you know that there will be a new board member orientation the morning of the first day. Remember to respond to all e-mails promptly, letting them know you will be there. If you are invited to bring a guest to the awards dinner, you need to let the board know of their attendance as well. Make sure you understand the dress code for all the meetings and events as well as the locations and times.

Take along a spiral notebook or journal designated just for the organization. Of course, taking notes electronically is just as effective as long as you keep them organized by date. You can note questions as well as action items for follow-up at a later date. Now let's discuss best practices indicative of a well-run board orientation and meeting.

Advance Reading Materials

In order for the board to conduct its business efficiently, it is critical that all board members receive background materials for items to be discussed in advance of the meeting. Sending materials electronically allows each member to download them on their flash drive or laptop so they can refer to them at the meeting. More and more boards are creating board-only websites where materials are posted, which will be discussed later in Chapter 10.

Your responsibility is to do your homework in advance of the meeting by reading the materials. Now is the time to raise any questions to the officer or committee chair who distributed the materials prior to the meeting. This helps the officer or chair understand any concerns that need to be addressed during the meeting. Particularly as a new board member, asking questions prior to the meeting allows you to get up to speed quickly and not take up everyone's time. There are no stupid questions, but some are best asked in private.

Typical Advance Reading Materials

Agenda

This should be formally approved at the start of the meeting. Sending it in advance allows participants to identify missing items or items that should be deleted because they are not ready for board discussion and action.

Minutes of the Previous Board Meeting

These will need to be approved at the meeting if they have not previously been approved. Since most boards vote to dispense with the reading of the minutes, it is imperative to send them in advance so any required changes can be proposed and incorporated prior to the meeting.

Executive Director Update

The CEO of the organization should keep the board informed of the activities of the staff, any issues, accomplishments, relevant statistics, and so on.

Financial Results

The treasurer or financial staff should provide the latest-available internal financial statements and the annual draft of the audited financial statements when they are available and ready for board acceptance. The financial results may also include investment reports reflecting asset allocation and summary performance compared to benchmarks (this will be discussed further in Chapter 5).

Development Activities and Results

This normally includes funds raised to date compared to the prior year as well as the results of any fund-raising events. Proposals for new development activities and events should include expected costs and amounts to be raised along with the *who* (target audience, staff involved, and board and committee involvement planned), *what*, *when*, and *where*'s for events.

Program Activities

In addition to the analysis of numbers served by the programs and a discussion of key success factors, any proposals for new programs should be provided. Proposals should include a complete discussion of what the goal of the new program is and how it will be executed, a budget, and its sources of funding.

Other Committee Reports

Instead of taking time during the meeting, committee chairs should update the board on their activities in writing in advance. Any board action needed should be specified and relevant information provided so that board members can come prepared to act.

Board Orientation

On arriving at your board orientation, you should have waiting for you a notebook or flash drive with key background information about the organization, including a current board list with names, titles, both work and home addresses (including e-mail addresses), and preferred contact phone numbers. The same should be provided for the staff. Other materials that may be provided include the following:

- Recent financial statements and/or the last-audited financial statements
- Literature about the organization that is used for development or programmatic purposes
- Recent newsletters or magazines published by the organization
- Calendar of events for the coming year
- Bylaws, articles of incorporation, standing rules, policies, and procedures
- Mission and strategic plan

The actual orientation is normally conducted by the officers, committee chairs, and key staff personnel and includes a "walk through" of the notebook/flash drive. A typical agenda for the orientation is as follows:

- History of the organization and its purpose or mission
- Discussion of the strategic plan and goals for the current year
- Review of the financial statements, including an explanation of fund accounting and the investing policies and procedures
- Key development activities, including major events

- Board expectations
- A presentation by each committee chair on what their committee is responsible for, including their focus for the coming year
- Introduction of key staff personnel who each explain their areas of responsibility

Most important, the orientation should include plenty of time for questions and answers. Hopefully, they will explain all those acronyms that every organization seems to create.

At the orientation you should be assigned a mentor to help guide you through your first year as a board member. Usually, this is someone with similar interests who has served on the board for a few years. A good mentor will perform the following:

- Ensure you are introduced during meetings and social functions
- Contact you regularly during the first year to answer questions and keep you informed
- Encourage you to be an active participant
- Survey you periodically to ensure board membership is meeting your expectations
- Report to the board chair variances between expectations and experience

By the end of the orientation you may feel a bit overwhelmed, but at least you now have some background and a mentor before going into your meetings. You may also have some idea of what committee(s) you would like to serve on. Since committee meetings are often held after the orientation but before the board meeting, you may want to sit in on whatever committee(s) you think you may be interested in.

Robert's Rules of Order

Most well-run organizations conduct their meetings in accordance with parliamentary procedure outlined in *The Eleventh Edition of Robert's Rules of Order Newly Revised*. Often an organization's bylaws specify that meetings and conventions be conducted in accordance with the latest edition of *Robert's Rules of Order*, which according to its website, http://www.roberts rules.com, "is the only book to have been maintained since 1876 under the continuing program established by General Henry M. Robert." Each board should have this reference available should a parliamentary question arise. In addition, now a short book is issued by the same publisher, entitled *Robert's Rule of Order Newly Revised in Brief*. It provides a summarized introduction to parliamentary procedure. The full edition is available on CD-ROM designed for installation on a laptop.

Familiarity with the basic parliamentary rules for meetings will make any new board member more comfortable in making motions, understanding when a "second" is required to a motion, understanding the rules of debate, and knowing how to end them by "calling for the question." All this sounds like a foreign language, but once you understand the basics as outlined in the aforementioned short book, you will understand how to take part in the meetings more effectively.

Often, action must be taken by a board in between scheduled in-person meetings. In today's environment of conducting electronic meetings and votes, parliamentary procedure can get more complicated. In addition, state law may establish guidelines for fax and other electronic voting. For example, currently in Ohio, fax votes require subsequent ratification at an in-person meeting. *Robert's Rules of Order* provides guidance and sample rules for electronic meetings.

The goal is to always keep a meeting orderly and efficient by keeping discussion on track, and *Robert's Rules of Order* is the best resource for doing so.

What Does Fiduciary Responsibility Mean?

Sometime during your orientation or your first meeting, someone may say something about exercising fiduciary responsibility or duty. This may be a new concept to you and is probably the most important guiding principle of board service. A board member should never do anything that is or may be perceived as violating fiduciary responsibility or duty. It is your responsibility as a board member to serve as a fiduciary of the organization to ensure to the best of your ability its long-term viability. The Cornell Law School Legal Information Institute website (http://www.law.cornell.edu/wex/fiduciary_duty) defines fiduciary duty as follows:

> A fiduciary duty is a legal duty to act solely in another party's interest. Parties owing this duty are called fiduciaries. The individuals to whom they owe a duty are called principals. Fiduciaries may not profit from their relationship with their principals unless they have the principals' express informed consent. They also have a duty to avoid any conflicts of interest between themselves and their principals or between their principals and the fiduciaries' other clients. A fiduciary duty is the strictest duty of care recognized by the US legal system.

In your situation as a board member, you are a fiduciary for the organization, which is the principal in the preceding definition. Whenever you are acting as a board member, you should ask yourself if you are acting solely for the benefit of the organization.

Conflict of Interest Statements

Annually each board member should sign a conflict of interest statement, which asks the board member to represent that they have no conflict of interest or asks them to list any potential conflicts of interest. For example, if your brother is a partner with the law firm the organization is using, that fact should be disclosed. Or if your wife is the partner responsible for the audit of the organization, independence rules prohibit you from serving on the board.

Some areas are gray and may just require disclosure, such as your employer having a bank loan to the organization. In that situation, and assuming you are not the direct lending officer, you can probably disclose the relationship and abstain from voting on matters related to loan acceptance.

A sample conflict of interest policy and annual statement from the IRS guidelines follows:

SAMPLE CONFLICT OF INTEREST POLICY AND ANNUAL STATEMENT

For Directors and Officers and Members of a Committee with Board Delegated Powers

Article I—Purpose

1. The purpose of this Board conflict of interest policy is to protect the organization's interests when it is contemplating entering into a transaction or arrangement that might benefit the private interests of an officer or director or might result in a possible excess benefit transaction.
2. This policy is intended to supplement, but not replace, any applicable state and federal laws governing conflicts of interest applicable to nonprofit and charitable organizations.
3. This policy is also intended to identify "independent" directors.

Article II—Definitions

1. **Interested Person**—Any director, principal officer, or member of a committee with governing board delegated powers, who has a direct or indirect financial interest, as defined below, is an interested person.
2. **Financial Interest**—A person has a financial interest if the person has, directly or indirectly, through business, investment, or family:

    a. An ownership or investment interest in any entity with which the organization has a transaction or arrangement,

b. A compensation arrangement with the organization or with any entity or individual with which it has a transaction or arrangement, or

c. A potential ownership or investment interest in, or compensation arrangement with, any entity or individual with which it is negotiating a transaction or arrangement.

Compensation includes direct and indirect remuneration as well as gifts or favors that are not insubstantial. A financial interest is not necessarily a conflict of interest. A person who has a financial interest may have a conflict of interest only if the Board or Executive Committee decides that a conflict of interest exists, in accordance with this policy.

3. **Independent Director**—A director shall be considered "independent" for the purposes of this policy if he or she is "independent" as defined in the instructions for the IRS 990 form or, until such definition is available, the director—

a. is not, and has not been for a period of at least three years, an employee of the organization or any entity in which it has a financial interest;

b. does not directly or indirectly have a significant business relationship with the organization, which might affect independence in decision-making;

c. is not employed as an executive of another corporation where any of the organization's executive officers or employees serve on that corporation's compensation committee; and

d. does not have an immediate family member who is an executive officer or employee of the organization or who holds a position that has a significant financial relationship with the organization.

Article III—Procedures

1. **Duty to Disclose**—In connection with any actual or possible conflict of interest, an interested person must disclose the existence of the financial interest and be given the opportunity to disclose all material facts to the Board or Executive Committee.

2. **Recusal of Self**—Any director may recuse himself or herself at any time from involvement in any decision or discussion in which the director believes he or she has or may have a conflict of interest, without going through the process for determining whether a conflict of interest exists.

3. **Determining Whether a Conflict of Interest Exists**—After disclosure of the financial interest and all material facts, and after any discussion

with the interested person, he/she shall leave the Board or Executive Committee meeting while the determination of a conflict of interest is discussed and voted upon. The remaining Board or Executive Committee members shall decide if a conflict of interest exists.

4. **Procedures for Addressing the Conflict of Interest**

   a. After exercising due diligence, the Board or Executive Committee shall determine whether the organization can obtain with reasonable efforts a more advantageous transaction or arrangement from a person or entity that would not give rise to a conflict of interest.

   b. If a more advantageous transaction or arrangement is not reasonably possible under circumstances not producing a conflict of interest, the Board or Executive Committee shall determine by a majority vote of the disinterested directors whether the transaction or arrangement is in the organization's best interest, for its own benefit, and whether it is fair and reasonable. In conformity with the above determination, it shall make its decision as to whether to enter into the transaction or arrangement.

5. **Violations of the Conflicts of Interest Policy**

   a. If the Board or Executive Committee has reasonable cause to believe a member has failed to disclose actual or possible conflicts of interest, it shall inform the member of the basis for such belief and afford the member an opportunity to explain the alleged failure to disclose.

   b. If, after hearing the member's response and after making further investigation as warranted by the circumstances, the Board or Executive Committee determines the member has failed to disclose an actual or possible conflict of interest, it shall take appropriate disciplinary and corrective action.

Article IV—Records of Proceedings

The minutes of the Board and all committees with board delegated powers shall contain:

a. The names of the persons who disclosed or otherwise were found to have a financial interest in connection with an actual or possible conflict of interest, the nature of the financial interest, any action taken to determine whether a conflict of interest was present, and the Board's or Executive Committee's decision as to whether a conflict of interest in fact existed.

b. The names of the persons who were present for discussions and votes relating to the transaction or arrangement, the content of the discussion, including any alternatives to the proposed transaction or arrangement, and a record of any votes taken in connection with the proceedings.

Article V—Compensation

a. A voting member of the Board who receives compensation, directly or indirectly, from the organization for services is precluded from voting on matters pertaining to that member's compensation.

b. A voting member of any committee whose jurisdiction includes compensation matters and who receives compensation, directly or indirectly, from the organization for services is precluded from voting on matters pertaining to that member's compensation.

c. No voting member of the Board or any committee whose jurisdiction includes compensation matters and who receives compensation, directly or indirectly, from the organization, either individually or collectively, is prohibited from providing information to any committee regarding compensation.

Article VI—Annual Statements

1. Each director, principal officer and member of a committee with Board delegated powers shall annually sign a statement which affirms such person:

    a. Has received a copy of the conflict of interest policy,

    b. Has read and understands the policy,

    c. Has agreed to comply with the policy, and

    d. Understands the organization is charitable and in order to maintain its federal tax exemption it must engage primarily in activities which accomplish one or more of its tax-exempt purposes.

2. Each voting member of the Board shall annually sign a statement which declares whether such person is an independent director.

3. If at any time during the year, the information in the annual statement changes materially, the director shall disclose such changes and revise the annual disclosure form.

4. The Executive Committee shall regularly and consistently monitor and enforce compliance with this policy by reviewing annual statements and taking such other actions as are necessary for effective oversight.

Article VII—Periodic Reviews

To ensure the organization operates in a manner consistent with charitable purposes and does not engage in activities that could jeopardize its tax-exempt status, periodic reviews shall be conducted. The periodic reviews shall, at a minimum, include the following subjects:

a. Whether compensation arrangements and benefits are reasonable, based on competent survey information (if reasonably available), and the result of arm's length bargaining.

b. Whether partnerships, joint ventures, and arrangements with manage-ment organizations, if any, conform to the organization's written policies, are properly recorded, reflect reasonable investment or payments for goods and services, further charitable purposes and do not result in inure-ment or impermissible private benefit or in an excess benefit transaction.

(Adapted from www.form1023.org, Sample Conflict of Interest Policy)

DIRECTOR AND OFFICER ANNUAL CONFLICT OF INTEREST STATEMENT

1. Name: _____   Date: _____

2. Position:

   Are you a voting Director? Yes No
   Are you an Officer? Yes No
   If you are an Officer, which Officer position do you hold:

   _____

3. I affirm the following:

   I have received a copy of the Conflict of Interest Policy.
   _____ (initial)
   I have read and understand the policy. _____ (initial)
   I agree to comply with the policy. _____ (initial)
   I understand that _____ is charitable and in order to main-tain its federal tax exemption it must engage primarily in activities which accomplish one or more of tax-exempt purposes.
   _____ (initial)

4. Disclosures:

   a. Do you have a financial interest (current or potential), including a compensation arrangement, as defined in the Conflict of Interest policy with _____? Yes No

      i. If yes, please describe it: _____

      _____

      ii. If yes, has the financial interest been disclosed, as provided in the Conflict of Interest policy? Yes No

   b. In the past, have you had a financial interest, including a compen-sation arrangement, as defined in the Conflict of Interest policy? Yes No

      i. If yes, please describe it, including when (approximately):

      _____

ii.   If yes, has the financial interest been disclosed, as provided in the Conflict of Interest policy? Yes No

5.   Are you an independent director, as defined in the Conflict of Interest policy? Yes No

a.   If you are not independent, why? _____

_____

Date: _____   Signature of Director: _____

Date of Review by Executive Committee: _____

So What Did You Think of Your First Meeting?

Your head might be spinning from all the meetings and events over the past few days. Hopefully you are also excited to be part of such a worthy organization and ready to jump in and get involved.

You may be asked to fill out an evaluation of the meetings and events. It is best to fill them out before you even leave the meeting while everything is fresh. In any event, when you get home or back to the office and as soon as you have a few moments, go back and review your notes. Assess how you think the meeting went. Here are a few questions that a strong board would ask itself:

- Was the meeting run in an organized, efficient fashion, with everyone having the opportunity to be heard but no one person or segment dominating discussion?
- If new members were in attendance, were they made to feel welcome, and did the orientation provide them the tools they needed to get involved?
- Were there opportunities such as icebreaker exercises or informal lunches or receptions to allow them to get to know each other?
- Was the focus on the goals for this year consistent with our strategic plan, or did we lose focus and perhaps get excited about the "flavor of the month" idea? If we are always focused on a new initiative, we will not accomplish anything. Are we following the plan so that by the end of the year we will accomplish our goals?
- Did we cover the right number of topics in the right depth to keep the board interested and engaged?
- Was business conducted at the right level? By that I mean, did the business merit board attention, or was it better addressed at the committee level or by

staff? I have to admit I am very sensitive to this one since I just spent an hour on a board conference call while they discussed what restaurant a certain event should be held at and what the menu should look like. Pure torture! The staff and the event committee should have handled this and presented it to the board for information and budget approval.

- Did we get the opportunity to hear from and interact with the key staff? While we want this opportunity, it is a board meeting, and the staff should not conduct or dominate the board meeting.

- Did I feel like we are getting the complete picture? Staff should tell the whole story and not just the good news. I need to know the issues that require board attention, both good and bad. Please do not put only the positive spin on everything.

- Did we get the opportunity to hear from and interact with beneficiaries of our programs? These opportunities keep us motivated.

- At the end of the meeting, did we feel exuberant or worn out? Because boards meet infrequently and try to squeeze so much in, the latter can happen. This is a situation where the executive committee, which includes the officers, needs to focus on having the committees take on more between meetings. Also, the agenda items and timing need to be reviewed to be sure there are plenty of breaks and no data overload.

Once you have asked yourself these questions, it may be time to have a conversation with a member of the executive committee or your mentor to raise any issues and ask questions. The easiest way to provide feedback and suggestions is on the evaluations, but if something strikes you later, just send an e-mail. A key benefit of having a new board member is having a fresh set of eyes and a new perspective. A strong executive committee will welcome your input.

Now look at the notes for next steps. Perhaps you were assigned to a committee. Make sure your calendar is updated for all meetings, conference calls, and events.

What to Expect Next

Just because the board meeting is over does not mean your work is done until the next meeting. Perhaps you were given a project or asked to research something. While you are excited, start the project or research. If you were given an assignment that is development related, go ahead and schedule that appointment or lunch. Once you get back to your normal day-to-day busy life, it is easy to let these volunteer obligations slip, so get them started now.

Either as a result of discussions at the board meeting or other circumstances, the board may need to take action in between meetings. The bylaws may permit action via a facsimile or electronic vote. Some state laws require that all votes taken electronically require a 100% response instead of the normal quorum unless the bylaws permit otherwise. In any event when you receive an electronic vote, ask questions of the chair or another officer if you are unclear and raise concerns, if necessary, just as you would in a regular board meeting. Once addressed to your satisfaction, return your vote in a timely fashion. Some states require that all votes taken electronically be ratified at the next regular, in-person board meeting.

Board meetings may also be held telephonically and generally require a shorter notice period. Usually they are called to address a specific issue that cannot wait until the next regular meeting. They should have an agenda and materials that are provided sufficiently in advance for board members to review and be prepared. A challenge for telephonic board meetings is to ensure everyone is heard without talking over each other. Always identify yourself when speaking so the other participants know who is speaking. Boards should be encouraged to use technology such as Zoom for these meetings so documents can be shared and video can be used.

Reality Check

My friend, Kathy, just called me. She is so frustrated. Last year she agreed to go on the board of trustees for her alma mater's School of Art Foundation. She had been active at the school since graduation and most recently had chaired its undergraduate advisory board. It was in that capacity that she had been asked to serve on the board of trustees in an ex officio capacity. I remember how excited she was when the school asked her to serve. The board had just concluded a campaign to build a new state-of-the-art (no pun intended) building, which is opening next month. The board includes the largest donor to the building, one of the most successful alumni of the school, as well as many other successful, well-known artists and businessmen. Getting to serve and interact with them is quite an honor.

In Kathy's first meeting, she was star struck since in addition to the meetings there was a dinner honoring an award-winning movie star alum. It was an eye-opening first meeting. She found out that while they had completed the campaign to construct the building, they had not found the funds to establish an endowment to maintain the building or to finish some of the classrooms. While there was a board-only website containing advance materials, it consisted of the previous meeting minutes in bullet point form, PowerPoint presentations from the previous meeting (pretty charts, but what do they really mean?), an agenda for the upcoming meeting, and a calendar of future meetings marked "tentative." There was no board orientation or mentor assigned to her, and she really did not feel close enough to any of the other board members to contact them. She felt they were just too busy.

The board met only twice a year, and the meetings primarily consisted of presentations by the dean and key faculty members on new initiatives, which all seemed to be great ideas but lacked funding for execution. The board did get to have dinner with some students and faculty. There were committees, but it seemed only the marketing committee and finance committee met because they were the most vocal in the meetings and in fact dominated the board portion of the meeting. There did not seem to be a strategic plan or focus since each meeting introduced new ideas with the goal of increasing the stature of the school and therefore the enrollment of its graduate programs, which were presented as paying for the rest of the operations, including the undergraduate programs. Kathy was suspicious of that since they did not receive any detailed financial information at the program level. Did I mention Kathy was an artist who paid the bills by being a certified public accountant? To make matters worse, since she was an "ex officio" member of the board, she was not sure of her role or if she even had a vote. The board did hand out meeting evaluations at the end of the meetings asking for ratings on each presentation.

Let's pause here—what do you think Kathy should do? What resources (besides me) might she draw on? How can she make a difference? She is committed to her alma mater. There are many right answers here and the only one wrong answer—giving up and resigning.

Epilogue

I suggested Kathy ask for a meeting with the dean. He was happy to meet with her. He listened to her questions and concerns, but he seemed overwhelmed and going in too many different directions. She did find out that they were hiring a part-time chief financial officer (CFO) for the school and were speaking with a fellow classmate who had recently retired. Her next step was to ask for a copy of the bylaws and check *Robert's Rules of Order* to determine that she did have a vote and could serve on committees. At the next meeting, she had the opportunity to spend time with and get to know some of the other board members who, like her, wanted to get more involved and had some of the same concerns she had. Together they approached the board chair who shared that he had been counseling the dean to be more focused and had suggested that a strategic planning process be undertaken jointly with the faculty and staff.

A few weeks later, Kathy got a call from the new CFO wanting to have lunch. She was in a panic and asked that Kathy keep their lunch meeting confidential. She had discovered that the financial situation was much more critical than anyone knew. If enrollment did not turn around, costs cut, and donations increased, it would be difficult to keep the doors open after the next year. She had a feeling that the dean had been afraid to share the full truth with the board. Kathy encouraged the CFO to share the financial results, including what she was able to compile at the program level. Hard decisions needed to be made, and there were a number of smart board members to make those decisions. But they needed the facts and complete picture. At the next meeting, the CFO presented the facts. Kathy and a few other board members were asked to serve on a task force to consider engaging a consultant to identify what needed to be done to ensure the financial sustainability of the school and start the strategic planning process. Understanding the need for urgency, the dean asked a key faculty member with prior corporate experience to begin meeting with the faculty to gather thoughts and information needed for the consultants and the strategic planning process. Stay tuned.

CHAPTER THREE

Board Governance

What Committee(s)
Should I Serve On?
What Is the Staff
versus Board Role?

Boards require a structure to carry out their purpose and vision. The formal structure of the board is defined in the bylaws or articles of incorporation of the organization. While titles may vary, each board needs certain officers. These officers consist of a chair or president, a secretary, and a treasurer. Beyond those officers, an organization may have a vice chair or vice president and/or a chair-elect. Often these positions serve as chair or president in the event that the elected chair or president is unable to serve either permanently or for a set meeting or event. The secretary is responsible for maintaining the records of the organization such as the minutes of the meetings and executing certain resolutions for matters such as the establishment of bank accounts. The treasurer is responsible for the financial assets and liabilities as well as for financial reporting. The treasurer is often the chair of the finance committee. While these positions are voluntary and elected, they carry a great deal of responsibility and often require an extensive time commitment. The officers are also members of the executive committee, which is empowered to act on behalf of the board and in between board meetings.

Additional officer positions may include specifically tasked vice presidents, such as a vice president for membership development, a vice president for programming, and a vice president for fund development. As part of the strategic planning process, the structure of the board should be evaluated, and positions should be eliminated if they are not needed. The roles and responsibilities for each officer position should be formally documented and evaluated regularly.

Board Rotation and Term Limits

In order to function effectively, boards need fresh perspectives as well as historical perspectives. Term limits should be long enough to allow members to thoroughly understand the organization and their roles but short enough to permit new ideas from new board members and avoid giving members concern over a long-term commitment. A model that often works well is a three-year term, with the option of reelection for an additional three-year term. This model also provides time for members to gain the knowledge to serve as officers.

Committee Structure

As a new board member, you may be asked what committees you have an interest in serving on, or you may be appointed to one or more committees where there is a particular need for your skill set. For example, if you have finance expertise, you will likely be asked to serve on the finance committee. In addition to standing committees that have continuing responsibilities, special committees or task forces, project teams, steering committees, or working groups may be appointed to address short-term issues and needs. A task force may be appointed to develop a plan to address a current issue, such as improving race relations. A project team may be appointed to oversee the renovation of a headquarters facility. A steering committee may be formed to plan for a special fund-raiser.

While committees have a longer-term focus and typically exist from year to year, their need, roles, and responsibilities should be evaluated annually. The bylaws or other governing documents may specify certain required committees. Typically, they may specify a Board Governance Committee with responsibilities for board and officer nominations. Also, they often require finance and audit committees. The creation of other committees may be the result of strategic planning or have evolved over the years. A best practice is to reevaluate the need for each committee and to set goals for the committee annually. Having committee meetings just to have meetings is a waste of everyone's valuable time.

The composition of a committee may be defined in the organization's governing documents as well. Each committee should have a charter that defines meeting frequency and whether the meetings have to be in person or can be held telephonically. The specific expertise or interest of a committee member should be discussed. The number of members and ex officio (defined as members who serve by virtue of their position) members, including whether they have a vote, should be delineated in the charter. Finally, the roles and responsibilities of the committee should be spelled out, as well as whether they can act in the absence of the board or take action on behalf of the board.

It is a good idea to permit nonboard members to serve on certain committees, both to gain additional expertise that may not be present on the board and to provide an opportunity to get to know prospective board members. Committee membership is a great way to engage interested parties and donors.

Board Committee Roles

Committees carry out the work that would not be efficient for the entire board to focus on. They often meet in between board meetings. Each committee's charter or job description defines the purpose of the committee, the duties and responsibilities delegated to the committee, its reporting requirements and deadlines, the staff assigned, and how the chair and any assistants are selected or appointed. The chairperson should be senior to most members and organized and should possess the leadership skills to bring the committee to a consensus while keeping the members focused on their priorities. The chair plans the meetings, consults with staff, provides an agenda, conducts the meetings, and ensures accurate minutes are kept, including any motions and recommendations to be carried to the full board. The chair reports on the committee's activities to the full board. Most important, the chair motivates the committee members to actively participate. Additional considerations for chairing a committee are discussed later in this chapter. The board chair may be an ex officio member of a committee and should have access to all committee minutes and records.

The charter or job description of the committee should be circulated to new board members so they can express an interest and match their skills or special knowledge to the committee requirements. Key components of a committee charter are as follows:

- Organization—who appoints the committee, the skill set required of committee members, how often they meet, how often they report to the board
- Purpose—defines the overall responsibilities of the committee (e.g., audit committee has oversight responsibility for the audit of the financial statements, including engagement of the audit firm, the effectiveness of internal controls, and compliance with laws and regulations)
- Duties and responsibilities—list the detailed responsibilities and the timeline for completion and reporting
- Authority—describes any actions authorized or delegated to the committee by the board
- Frequency of the review of the charter and date adopted

Committees should be composed of a diverse group of participants to ensure different perspectives. The committee descriptions discuss who should serve on the different examples of committees.

Why Are Some Committees More Fun Than Others?

After you have the job description and meet the committee chairperson, how will you choose what committee to serve on? Certainly, your skill set will point you in a direction. Observe the committees in action by sitting in on a couple different committee meetings before deciding. How passionate and engaged are the committee members? How well does the chairperson work with the committee? Is the chairperson organized, and does the chairperson ensure everyone gets a chance to speak? Does it seem like they are enthusiastic and accomplish something at every meeting? Think about why you agreed to join the board and what facet of the organization you are most passionate about. The committee that has the responsibility for that facet is where you belong.

Representative Types of Committees

Executive Committee

Acts on behalf of the board in between board meetings as provided for in the organizational documents such as the bylaws.

Meets more frequently than the board to address matters that need to be addressed in between board meetings. For example, the approval of the budget or a contract agreement may be delegated to the executive committee.

Serves as a sounding board for the officers allowing them to raise issues and obtain feedback prior to presentation to the entire board.

Assists the chair in developing the agenda for the board meetings and often meets just prior to the board meeting to discuss topics that will be addressed in the board meeting.

May be authorized to appoint a member to the board in the event of an unexpected vacancy (depends on board organizational documents).

Who should serve on this committee?

Each of the officers should serve on the executive committee. Others who often serve are the chairs of the standing committees who may serve with or without a vote. However, if they do not have a vote, they may wonder why they serve on the committee. Some executive committees also include the immediate past president or chair. The chair may have the right to appoint other board members to at-large seats on the executive committee. Ideally, the executive committee is representative of the entire board. The executive director of the organization is the staff liaison for this committee.

Board Governance

Oversees the nomination process for both new board members and board officers.

Is generally responsible for orientation, training, and mentor programs for new board members.

Conducts the evaluation of board meetings and individual board members.

Recommends revisions to policies and governing documents as necessary to ensure efficient and effective board performance.

Who should serve on this committee?

Because this committee is responsible for recommending new board members, this committee should be representative of your organization. Those who serve should be well connected with your organization's community of stakeholders since that is your pool of candidates. While experienced board members have the best understanding of the various roles within the board and committee needs, it is suggested to have one relatively new member to bring fresh thoughts. Those who understand nonprofit statutes and governance rules such as lawyers often are needed on this committee. The board chair as well as the executive director should be ex officio on this very important committee.

Budget and Finance

Reviews the annual budget and presents it to the board for approval.

Monitors financial performance against that budget and ensures accurate financial reporting to the board.

Reviews risk and internal controls to safeguard assets and determine that appropriate accounting procedures are used.

Reviews legal requirements such as debt and regulatory compliance.

Who should serve on this committee?

This committee has one of the most technical skill set requirements in that everyone on the committee should have a working knowledge of finances. While they do not need to be certified public accountants, they do need to know how to read the financial statements, develop and work with budgets, and work with banks and regulatory authorities in certain situations. They need to be financially literate and respectful of deadlines. The board treasurer should serve on this committee and may be the chair. The staff person responsible for the finances of the organization should be the staff liaison.

Audit

Is responsible for the engagement of the auditors for the annual audit.

Conducts the selection process for the audit and tax firm or firms.

Meets with auditors and reviews the draft financial statements, the tax reporting, and the required communications from the auditors, including the management letter documenting internal control weaknesses and other recommendations.

Drafts and reviews audit committee charter annually.

In the event of fraud or illegal acts may be asked to oversee the investigation and engage professionals to investigate.

Who should serve on this committee?

Here it would be helpful to have a current or retired certified public accountant with audit and tax experience and/or an internal auditor for another organization. The members must all understand how to read financial statements and respect the importance of internal controls.

Investment

Is responsible for oversight of the investment assets of the organization.

Engages investment consultants and investment managers.

Creates the investment policy in order to maximize return while minimizing risk.

Reviews investment reports and recommends spending policy based on expected investment results.

Monitors compliance with investment policy.

Who should serve on this committee?

Ideally, the members should have investing experience for more than their personal accounts. A current or retired investment advisor is most qualified. If investments are significant, the committee should comprise investment experts in the various types or classes of investments such as equities, debt, and alternatives such as real assets or hedge funds. In Chapter 5, we will discuss the importance of diversification in the organization's investments. That diversification expertise should also be included on the committee. There was a situation where the only investment expertise on the investment committee was a local stockbroker. He suggested the organization invest only in the equities of a few large corporations. When the stock market took a dive, so did the investments of the organization. The staff liaison should be the person responsible for investments. As mentioned later, the organization's investment consultant will be a regular participant as well.

Communications/Branding/Marketing

Is responsible for ensuring that the brand, image, and mission of the organization are properly reflected in all communication materials.

Reviews the style guide to help ensure consistent brand messaging.

Makes recommendations as to frequency and nature of communications to ensure the stakeholders, including members, donors and potential donors, and beneficiaries, all understand the excitement and culture of the organization.

Who should serve on this committee?

Here is where you want your creative thinkers. The best members are those with experience in journalism, marketing, media especially social media, and public relations. It is important to have a good cross-section of ages represented. Different generations prefer communication in different formats and mediums. As more and more communication is done via social media, committee members should include those who are active on social media. The staff liaison is the person responsible for communication and publications for the organization.

Programming

Oversees the creation of new programs consistent with the mission and strategic vision.

Ensures there is a methodology for evaluating programs and determining whether they should be continued.

Receives regular reports on the participation and results of programs.

Who should serve on this committee?

On this committee you should include those who have been served by the organization. For example, the programming committee for Virginia Special Olympics included parents of the athletes. Often those most passionate about the organization want to serve on this committee. You want both passion and innovative thinking. Programming needs to be continuously improved and kept fresh. Your committee members should be entrepreneurial thinkers willing to try new ideas, being open to calculated risks. They need to be collaborative and work well with staff. Creativity is a plus on this committee as well. Often this is considered one of the "fun" committees, but you need committee members who not only can think big but also are realistic and willing to patiently evaluate those big ideas. Staff liaison is the programming director.

Special Events

Is responsible for specific events such as a fund-raising event or homes tour.

Recommends a budget for the event.

Ensures smooth execution of the event through planning and organization.

Evaluates success of the event both financially and from an engagement/partici-
     pation perspective.

Who should serve on this committee?

This is also often a popular committee that requires creativity as well as hard work during the period of the event. Continuity is important here as well as new board members for fresh ideas. Depending on the nature of the events, members need to understand the time commitment required during the planning and the event, ensuring they are available for that time frame. Organization skills are important as well as collaboration skills. The ability to recruit and motivate volunteers is a required skill. The staff liaison is the programming staff responsible for events.

Development or Fund-Raising

Is responsible for working with staff to raise the funds to ensure the financial
     stability of the organization.

Motivates the board to make their financial commitment to the organization.

Who should serve on this committee?

This is sometimes one of the hardest committees to recruit for. As discussed Chapter 4, fund-raising is often "friend raising," so members should be well connected, strong personal donors and comfortable in the solicitation role once trained. One major foundation decided the entire board should serve as the development committee. It made it clear that every board member needed to raise funds for the foundation, both personally and through their network. A willingness to hold other board members accountable and strong follow-up skills are required. The vice president for development is the staff liaison.

Membership (for Organizations That Are Membership Organizations)

Responsible for evaluating applications for membership and selection of new
     members.

Responsible for the application process and defining the requirements for membership, including different classes of membership, if applicable.

Conducts membership campaigns or other recruiting efforts to ensure growth in members.

Evaluates and communicates the benefits of membership.

Who should serve on this committee?

Those most passionate about the organization are the best committee members since their enthusiasm is contagious. One organization had the former board chair move into the chair of the membership committee at the conclusion of his term as board chair. He was excellent at explaining the benefits of membership through stories and testimonies. Since organizations strive for diverse members, the committee should also be diverse in gender, age, and ethnicity. Consider who has been a strong recruiter for the organization and ask them to serve on this committee. The staff responsible for membership is the liaison.

Capital Planning

Is responsible for planning and overseeing capital projects and may be involved in lease negotiations.

Develops a master capital plan and prepares a multiyear budget for capital projects.

Who should serve on this committee?

The best members of this committee are often those with facilities maintenance, leasing, construction, and real estate experience. They need to understand project management and financing. The staff liaison is normally the person responsible for the organization's facilities, but for major projects, the executive director will want to be involved.

Personnel/Human Resources

Ensures that personnel policies are developed and complied with.

Is responsible for hiring and evaluating the executive director of the organization.

May review benefit plans and other compensation arrangements.

Who should serve on this committee?

Those who have served their companies as a human resource officer are key to the success of this committee. Employment lawyers may also be a strong asset to the committee. Compassionate good listeners are important to all the committees but especially to this committee.

The aforementioned list is not all-inclusive but rather describes some of the typical committees an organization may have.

Chairing a Committee

The chair of the committee has numerous responsibilities that are discussed further in Chapter 11. However, one of the first responsibilities of a new committee chair or a board member considering taking on the role of chair should be to ensure there is a position description for the chair. The chair should ensure the committee has a charter that, as previously discussed, describes the responsibilities of the committee. The prospective chair should understand the demands of the role as it relates to both the time required and the activities that involve the committee.

Key considerations for both a prospective committee member and the chair:

- How often does the committee meet?
- What technical skills are needed?
- What other groups does this committee interact with? What other groups should they interact with?
- Is the purpose of the committee clear and understood by staff and the board?

The chair should conduct further analysis working with the chair of the board. For example, consider how board meeting time should be used to more effectively support the goals of the committee. What reporting is expected from the committee? If resources were not an issue, what could the committee do to support the goals and vision of the organization? Are there tasks currently assigned that should not be and are there tasks that should be assigned to the committee? Would the committee benefit from a subcommittee or task force of a smaller group? Is there a committee member orientation, and how can it be improved? As with every leadership role on the board, the chair should evaluate committee members for succession planning. Putting someone in the role of committee vice chair may lead to a smoother transition.

Task Forces

Task forces may be formed to evaluate and make recommendations to the board relative to a specific short-term situation. These may be formed by the board or a committee. For example, the finance committee may form a task force to evaluate increasing dues, or the program committee may form a task force to identify award recipients. Task forces can also include nonboard members in order to broaden perspectives. Because they are formed for a specific purpose, their timeline must be clearly defined, and then they should be held accountable for meeting that deadline.

Volunteer–Staff Relationships

Strong committee and board performance result from a partnership between staff and volunteer board members. Effective organizations have a clear understanding of their respective roles as they move the organization forward. To be clear, the only staff member who reports directly to the board is the executive director.

Executive Director

Generally, the board is responsible for hiring the executive director, providing feedback to the executive director, communicating expectations, conducting annual personnel evaluations, and rewarding their performance. When external issues arise, the board has the role of analyzing the situation and working with the executive director to handle public relations and respond as one voice supporting the executive director.

In particular, executive directors of affiliated organizations may be in difficult situations. The administration of the related entity, such as a university, may see itself as the administrator of the affiliated foundation. Often, it is important to maintain separate control and oversight, which is why the independent foundation was established, even though it exists solely to benefit the university. The board chair may need to communicate with the related entity's administration that the executive director reports only to the foundation's board and is not to be directed by the related entity. Board chairs sometimes need to run interference for the executive director.

Staff–Volunteer Communication

The key to success in the leadership team of the executive director and the board is the ability to understand the expectations of each other and to communicate frequently. Joint responsibilities include establishing the priorities of the organization based on the overall strategic plan. They also include defining the *who*, *what*, *when*, *where*, and *how*'s of execution of the priorities. Jointly evaluating the activities and results is also important. Was the latest project worth the effort?

If regular communication is not planned, it tends to be infrequent. The board and staff need to agree on frequency, level of detail, and method of communication. Technology today facilitates communication, but it is important to understand each other's needs. Yes, there are board members who still do not use e-mail, text messaging, Dropbox, or whatever application is in vogue.

Setting up weekly or monthly calls with the appropriate staff member (board chair with executive director, committee chair with staff liaison) helps ensure accountability and progress. Effective teamwork requires relationship development. The best way to build relationships is to spend time together, even if it is telephonically. No surprises build trust. Things will not always go as planned, but if the board member is kept informed, both parties can use their specialized knowledge to resolve issues together.

Respect

Volunteers have much to learn from staff, and staff have much to learn from volunteers. Each is in their position because of their specialized experience, knowledge, and skills. Many board members have experiences gained in the for-profit world that are applicable in the nonprofit world. However, board members need to understand that that they are not the CEO/CFO or chief anything of the nonprofit and that the organization's staff are not their staff. They do not exist to serve the immediate needs of the board member. Staff need to understand how to relate to and manage volunteers, who are regularly turning over. Staff voice needs to be heard in committee meetings but should not direct the committee. Staff should speak out when they have clarifying data, when a decision has not considered the available resource constraints, and when there

Table 3.1

Board Responsibilities	Staff Responsibilities
Manages the strategic decision-making process	Provides information to assist in the decision-making process
Reviews data	Gathers, analyzes, and presents data
Sets priorities and establishes goals and objectives	Develops action plans to implement goals and objectives
Establishes relationships and seeks support from external stakeholders such as donors and related organizations	Provides research and document results of those solicitations and relationships
Evaluates risk and review policies and procedures for compliance with legal and regulatory requirements	Establishes procedures and systems for carrying out activities
Approves budgets	Recommends allocation of resources
Monitors progress and quality of programmatic and administrative support activities	Directs day-to-day operations
Recruits, motivates, and thanks volunteers	Supervises staff and volunteers
Establishes criteria for measuring the effectiveness and efficiency of the activities	Presents data and recommends revisions to programming

is a conflict with policy. Mutual respect is critical for a successful committee and staff partnership. Both groups are passionate about the mission of the organization, and only by working together can they fulfill the mission.

Succession Planning

Gaining the knowledge to serve as a board officer does not happen without well-thought-out succession planning. Even in the first year of board service, it can become apparent as to who has the enthusiasm, leadership skills, and time bandwidth to be considered for a future board leadership role. For example, the current board treasurer, knowing who has financial expertise, should observe and spend time with those new board members, explaining the finances of the organization. Then they can be encouraged to join the finance committee.

One of the primary responsibilities of board officers and committee chairs should be to identify and mentor their successor. Observing how engaged members are on a committee can help gauge level of interest and whether they have the time to take on additional responsibility. Perhaps if they appear to be a good prospect for a greater role, they can be assigned a project leadership role or asked to chair a task force. The leader needs to spend time with each potential board leader, explaining what is involved, the vision or charter for the committee, and time commitment required. They have to walk a fine line though because there are no guarantees the prospective leader will be ultimately selected. The organization may want to send multiple board members to leadership training to ensure there is a pool of possible future board officers.

In particular, vice presidents need to understand that no decision as to their becoming president was made when they were elected as vice president of the organization. The president should mentor the vice president(s) and share knowledge but, unless the role is defined as president-elect, the committee responsible for officer nominations, should evaluate all the board leadership for the role of president. Too often expectations are not set, feelings get hurt, and a valued board member is lost because they feel passed over. Situations and needs of the organization change, and the nominating committee may select someone they believe more suited for the role at that time.

Reality Check

We finally completed our strategic planning process. Out of that process came a new committee structure. We also decided that, due to an attendance/participation issue with about 20% of the board, we needed to increase the size of the board. Therefore, we had six new board members and two new committees, in addition to the three continuing committees—still a

fresh start. As a new board president, I was enthusiastic. I selected committee chairs who were all active, thoughtful participants in our board meetings.
I selected the investment banker as chair of the finance and investment committee. I selected the most thought-provoking corporate executive for chair
of the events committee. I selected the college professor who always focused
on inclusivity for volunteer management/regional engagement. That left
communications/marketing where I selected a private school fund-raiser.
I really wanted an experienced board member for board development, so
I selected a retired government administrator. All willingly agreed to serve as
chairs. The executive director selected the appropriate staff liaisons. I asked
the remaining board members to self-select two committees they were interested in serving on and then, based on skill set, appointed them to one of
their two choices. New board members heard from the chairs about what the
committees did during their orientation and had the opportunity to sit in on
a committee meeting during their first board meeting weekend. Each committee was given their portion of the strategic plan and asked to work with
staff to develop tasks around the goals and objectives and then regularly
report to the board in advance of each board meeting. It sounds great and
initially was great. But then attendance at telephonic committee meetings
started dropping off. Meetings were not getting scheduled except when committee chairs knew they had to report at an upcoming board meeting. Staff
were having to organize the meetings and contact the committee members
over and over again to see if they were going to attend. I was perplexed—
what happened?

Well, several things did. We had recruited the "cream of the crop" to our
new board members, top-level executives and officials. They were busy people and, even though the expectations were made clear that committee service was an important part of their board responsibilities, they did not make
them a priority. One of the chairs got a promotion and never seemed to have
the time to organize the committee meetings. One of the chairs had the time
but did not have the knowledge of best practices for her committee, so staff
took over. Clear committee job descriptions incorporating the strategic priorities for the committee were never drafted, so some committees got too far
into operations, while others couldn't figure out what they should do.

How did we resolve these issues? We had to change out the committee
chair whose professional life did not allow her to do a good job as committee
chair. She was relieved because the stress was killing her. She went back to
being a wonderful asset to the committee. Committee job descriptions were
drafted, and goals and objectives from the strategic plan were clarified and
adjusted. Board training on best practices was implemented. Finally, time
was allotted at every board meeting for committees to meet. Relationships
among committee members developed as they met face to face. It is harder to
"blow off" a meeting if you know you are letting friends down.

CHAPTER FOUR

How to Be Comfortable Raising Funds for Your Organization

Most of us are not comfortable raising funds for our organization. We think of fund-raising as asking our friends and colleagues for major donations. Yet all of our organizations are dependent on donations for financial survival. Bake sales, raffles, dinners, home tours, and other events might be fun and generate good publicity, but they take a great deal of effort and normally do not generate substantial funds. This chapter discusses ways to generate resources and the steps for high-impact fund-raising. Finally, it discusses the various roles board members can play in generating funds (in addition to making personal donations). This effort requires the time, talent, and treasure of each board member like no other.

Giving is showing you care about the organization and its mission. As a board member you are modeling that you care. Just sharing that passion and how you share it impact your ability to get others to join you in giving. Just sharing the facts is not as effective as a personal story about, for example, the impact the organization had on your child's life. Stories and videos share the emotion and passion. There is a saying about leaders that applies here—"People don't care about how much you know. They care about how much you care." When a board member asks for a gift to their organization, they are asking the donor to join them in caring.

Table 4.1 summarizes all the different ways a person can show they care. It is intended to be a simple guide to fund-raising activities and the pros and cons of those activities.

Table 4.1

Ways to Raise Money	Example(s)	Pros	Cons
Event fees	Awards dinner where attendees pay $1,000 to attend.	Good publicity, venue for promoting all the good the organization does.	Requires substantial effort and costs; not fully tax deductible by attendees.
Event sponsorships	XYZ Corporation–sponsored athletic event.	Larger amounts raised with less effort. Donor gets promotional benefits. Because amounts are known in advance of events, it reduces financial stress.	Provides tickets or entertainment space to sponsor, reducing event revenue; must prepare and submit proposals well in advance of event in order to meet sponsor's budget timing.
Direct mail, e-mail, social media, or telephonic solicitation	Household mailings, telemarketer calls, crowdfunding on social media.	A good source of information on accuracy of potential donor data; easy and can be outsourced; generates smaller dollars but larger number of gifts.	Can be impersonal; low response rates result in a high cost per solicitation; may have to offer a solicitation premium to inspire response. Telemarketers have a poor reputation. Most states require registration prior to conducting solicitations.
Sell stuff	Girl Scout Cookies or museum shop.	Quality products generate good publicity; opportunity to explain the impact of profits from sales.	Requires a network and store or website location to generate sales; requires staff to buy and merchandise products; requires an investment in inventory.
Major gift solicitation	Engages high-capacity donors and asks for major gifts.	Results in larger gifts for the effort.	Needs data to identify and invest in cultivation of potential donors.

Major campaign (see Reality Check later)	Multiyear, campaign with specific dollar goal and identified needs.	Focused approach for a specific time period that can generate significant funds.	Staff and consultants required as well as case statement materials, all of which require an up-front investment.
Planned giving	Gifts from charitable trusts as well as estate gifts.	Somewhat easier to ask for since donor may retain certain rights and use of assets; can be modified and can be directed to a specific purpose.	Requires donor education and legal advice—receipt timing is unknown since have to wait for estates to "mature."
Naming opportunities	For contributing a large amount, the room/building/scholarship fund will bear donor's name.	Appeals to major donors; good way to raise funds for capital projects.	Difficult to establish "value."
Auctions—live, silent, raise the paddle	Donors contribute items or services that are auctioned off at an event; donors raise their bid paddles to donate outright a certain amount for the cause.	Can be fun and raise significant funds. Competitiveness among donors will increase bids and amounts raised.	Staff intensive; usually done in conjunction with another event.

Culture of Philanthropy

Does your organization have a culture of philanthropy where the entire board, volunteers, staff, and donors all understand that fund-raising is a year-round engagement effort? No matter what their roles, do they understand that every interaction has a development impact? As soon as anyone gets involved with the organization, do they understand the importance of personal giving at some level and that no gift is too small? Universities were a bit late in emphasizing that giving should begin when students are in their first year. It is much easier to move a donor up the gift levels if they start young and embrace their responsibility to give back.

Steps for High-Impact Fund-Raising

When you think about what organizations you give to, it is likely you are engaged with them. People give when they feel an emotional appeal or memories are evoked. Step one has to be developing a relationship with a potential donor. They are much more likely to give if you have engaged them somehow—visits from board members and staff, attendance at activities or events, even just reading your blog or magazine. You need to communicate that you consider them investors with shared values.

Popular today with many educational institutions and other nonprofits are days of giving. Here the emphasis is on participation by making any-size gift on that day rather than major gifts. However, major donors are often asked to provide matching gifts as incentives to encourage giving. The successful days of giving combine fun engagement activities, including get-togethers with day-long updates on progress toward both participation and dollar goals. Technology has impacted the ability to accept and report gifts in real time. Make sure your systems, particularly the website, can handle the significant increase in activity on that day. There may be competitions among organizations in the community, with the organization having the largest number of gifts or funds raised, receiving a bonus donation. The major benefit to days of giving is gaining new, often younger, donors that can then be incorporated into the organization's culture of giving.

Donors today want to understand what impact their gift will have. Those who ask for donations must be equipped with a short, sharp sales pitch describing the impact the organization is having. Testimonials from students who received scholarships and went on to specific great achievements are examples of sharing the impact. Share your own testimonial as to why you are involved and engaged. Donors like to give to organizations that are on an upward trajectory and not because you have a great need for funds. They want to invest in success stories.

Donors need to understand the vision for the organization and values. They want transparency and accountability. For example, is there an annual report that succinctly explains your sources and uses of funds? Does that report focus on the impact your programs are having? Donors need to consider their gift an investment in the cause. They need to be comfortable in the sustainability of the organization.

You may get asked about board participation in giving. Every board member should give to the extent they are able. Many boards have minimum giving levels. Especially in peer-to-peer solicitation, you want to ask them to join you in giving to the organization.

Board members and key volunteers can play key roles in building relationship and ultimately increasing funds raised. The donor development process starts with identifying potential significant donors. You may know they recently sold their business or are starting their estate planning process, so let your organization's development office know. Once donors' capacity is estimated, you can assist with the development of a strategy to build the relationship and identify what areas they are passionate about. You may be the best one to cultivate the relationship by inviting them to events or introducing development officers to them. Cultivation discussions also uncover shared values. Once meetings occur, you may be the best one to follow up with the donor and see if the gift proposal was appealing to them. Make sure you get information to the staff and into the database from cultivation interaction.

You may sense it is time to make the ask. If you are comfortable making an ask, utilize the information provided by staff to ask at the right level for the right-impact area so you are more likely to get a "yes." Choose a comfortable, private, convenient place to make the ask. Ask open-ended questions such as how they got involved with the organization. Follow that with a discussion on the particular program you think they might like to support. Finally, ask for a specific amount and then let it sink in (i.e., be silent). They may ask questions or ask for some follow-up information, which is good. It means they are giving the ask serious consideration. You may get some objections that you should address in a nonconfrontational way by listening with understanding and asking for clarification. If the amount is the issue, then ask how much they would be willing to give.

One approach might be a pre-proposal where you ask for their thoughts on a certain project and level of donation. Or you could say something like, "The executive director said you were interested in funding a scholarship. Is that where you would like to direct a gift?" If you approach it as helping them decide, involving them and facilitating their thinking, it becomes more of a conversation and less of a solicitation. Be a good listener and work to solve issues they may raise. You may not get the deal closed, but you will have gathered information to help move it forward and build the critical relationship.

Personal "thank-you's" go a long way in stewarding donors and in retaining them as donors. Some organizations ask board members to write personal thank-you notes to all donors contributing above a certain amount.

These acknowledgments should always express the impact their gift has or will have on achieving the organization's mission.

Since it takes more effort to get that first gift than to obtain subsequent gifts, it is important to understand why donors stop giving. Often it is because they do not receive measured results in their acknowledgment. They want a meaningful acknowledgment promptly and a report on what happened with their last gift. Over-solicitation, where a donor is asked to give again before they are satisfied with what was done with the last gift, is also cited as a reason for not giving.

Which Role in Fund-Raising Do You Want to Play?

Kay Sprinkel Grace in her book *The AAA Way to Fundraising Success: Maximizing Involvement, Maximizing Results* (Whit Press, 2009) suggests that a board is given an AAA rating in cases where every board member is motivated to be an ambassador, advocate, and/or asker. She defines these roles as follows:

- Ambassador

    - Has made a financial commitment to the organization
    - Cultivates prospective donors and stewards repeat donors
    - Must be informed and know the core values, vision, and priorities of the organization
    - Helps identify prospects
    - Invites prospective and existing donors to events

- Advocate

    - Has made a financial commitment to the organization
    - Shares information about the organization at every opportunity
    - May also serve as an advocate formally, making key presentations on the impact the organization has had on the community and its members
    - Must be informed and know the core values, vision, and priorities of the organization
    - May host an event
    - May represent the organization at community events

- Asker

    - Has made a financial commitment to the organization
    - Enjoys sharing their enthusiasm for the organization and asking for an investment
    - Well informed and well trained

- "Matched" with prospective donors or current donors for maximum possibility of success
- May be teamed with another board "asker" or staff member
- Staff organizes the ask so the asker's focus can be on the single purpose of getting or renewing the gift
- Willing to lend their name and sign letters asking for appointments or gifts
- Willing to seek sponsorships for events

With training and experience, board members may move from being an ambassador to being an advocate to being an asker. This is an area where the professional development staff can assist with training and ensure that the board member is comfortable with their role. Just accompanying the staff on a call to a potential donor allows the board member to observe the process of cultivation and stewardship. It may be helpful to survey the board members to determine what role they are comfortable with and within that role what specific tasks they would agree to perform.

Gift Planning

Unless you are a trust and estates attorney, your eyes may glaze over when development staff start discussing deferred giving. As a board member, you need to understand the basic concepts and why this may represent a significant opportunity for funds development. Table 4.2 outlines the common types of planned gifts. For each type of gift, the donor can specify how their gift should be used or leave it unrestricted.

Since tax laws change, a donor should consult their tax advisor before completing a planned gift. There may be tax implications that negate the benefits noted earlier. Table 4.2 is not providing tax advice but is only indicative of possible tax implications. If planned giving is going to be a significant development opportunity for the organization, it is likely going to be advantageous to hire legal expertise either in-house or outsourced to ensure donors' questions can be answered and they are comfortable with their decision.

Donor's Bill of Rights

The American Association of Fund Raising Counsel, the Association of Fundraising Professionals, the Association for Healthcare Philanthropy, and the Council for Advancement and Support of Education created the Donor's Bill of Rights. Each board member should be familiar with the Donor's Bill of Rights to ensure their organization is in compliance. Specifically, the Bill of Rights states the following: (*continues on p. 52*)

Table 4.2

Type	Description	Benefits to Donor
Gift from will or trust	Bequest that is unrestricted or directed to a specific purpose. It may be an amount or percentage of the balance remaining in an estate.	Donor retains control of assets. Bequest can be modified; may reduce the taxes that will have to be paid on the estate.
Gifts from a retirement plan	Organization is named as a beneficiary of an IRA, 401K or other qualified plan.	Can designate all or a portion by completing plan's beneficiary form; does not affect lifetime withdrawals; avoids double taxation since it is not part of the estate; designation can be modified.
Charitable gift annuity	Assets such as cash or appreciated securities are transferred to the organization. The organization pays the donor or their designee a fixed and guaranteed income for life. The remaining balance passes to the organization when the contract ends at the death of the last annuitant. Usually there is a minimum gift level and a minimum age to make it worth the effort to maintain.	Guaranteed, fixed income is received for life by donor or designee. A tax deduction for a portion of the gift is received by the donor. Earnings/annuity may be greater than the donor could earn individually.
Deferred gift annuity	Similar to charitable gift annuity but the annuity starts at a future time specified by donor, thereby increasing the annuity.	The deferral creates a larger tax deduction. Donor can start receiving payments when they want to, such as on retirement.
Charitable remainder unitrust	Assets such as cash, securities, or real estate are transferred into a trust. The trust pays a percentage of the value of the trust principal to the donor or their designee. The remainder passes to the organization when donor passes and trust terminates. Due to administrative costs, there is normally a minimum gift amount.	Donor or designee receives income and an immediate charitable tax deduction for a portion of the contribution to the trust. There are no up-front capital gains taxes on appreciated assets donated. Additional assets can be added to the trust.

Charitable lead trust	Assets are contributed to a trust that makes fixed annual payments to the organization. When the trust terminates, the remaining principal is paid to the donor's heirs.	Reduces estate and transfer taxes.
Retained life estate	Donor's personal real estate is deeded to the organization. Donor gets to continue to live in the home for life while maintaining it. On donor's passing, organization may sell or use the real estate as it chooses.	Donor receives a tax deduction for the fair market value of the real estate at the time of transfer, and no capital gains tax is paid.
Charitable bargain sale	Donor sells real estate to the organization for a price below the appraised market value. Organization usually then sells it and uses the proceeds for the specified gift purpose.	Donor receives immediate tax deduction for the difference between the amount the donor received and the appraised market value. No capital gains tax is paid on the donated portion of the property.

Source: William & Mary Office of University Advancement. www.wm.edu/giving/giftplanning

Philanthropy is based on voluntary action for the common good. It is a tradition of giving and sharing that is primary to the quality of life. To ensure that philanthropy merits the respect and trust of the general public, and that donors and prospective donors can have full confidence in the nonprofit organizations and causes they are asked to support, we declare that all donors have these rights:

- To be informed of the organization's mission, of the way the organization intends to use donated resources, and of its capacity to use donations effectively for their intended purposes.
- To be informed of the identity of those serving on the organization's governing board, and to expect the board to exercise prudent judgment in its stewardship responsibilities.
- To have access to the organization's most recent financial statements.
- To be assured their gifts will be used for the purposes for which they were given.
- To receive appropriate acknowledgement and recognition.
- To be assured that information about their donation is handled with respect and with confidentiality to the extent provided by law.
- To expect that all relationships with individuals representing organizations of interest to the donor will be professional in nature.
- To be informed whether those seeking donations are volunteers, employees of the organization or hired solicitors.
- To have the opportunity for their names to be deleted from mailing lists that an organization may intend to share.
- To feel free to ask questions when making a donation and to receive prompt, truthful and forthright answers.

State Registration Requirements for Charitable Solicitation

Most (currently 41) states require an organization to register and pay a fee prior to soliciting funds from individuals within their state. Registration is required for any solicitation, verbal or written or using technology, and includes events that include programs as well as a request for funds at any level. Penalties can be significant if your organization is not registered or has let its registration lapse. Unfortunately, each state has different requirements, but frequently they include a registration form signed by the board chair and/or treasurer, a copy of the audited financial statements, and a copy of the organization's Form 990. Registration renewal or annual reporting is required after the initial registration. Specialized service providers will maintain and file the registrations on behalf of the organizations for a fee that can be several thousand dollars. If your organization is required to file in every state, it may be worth it.

In addition, any paid professional fund-raiser hired to assist an organization with fund-raising activities may be required to register before assisting the nonprofit organization. The regulations are complicated, and unanswered questions are particularly related to solicitation via the Internet or social media. It is best to read the state's website for the agency that regulates fund-raising. Some states require a disclosure statement to be included on written solicitations and/or acknowledgments. There are exemptions in most states for certain educational institutions and religious congregations as well as for membership organizations who only solicit their members.

The states the organization is registered in are required to be listed on Form 990. Because of the complexity of the requirements, it is best to consult legal counsel when addressing this issue. As a board member you are responsible for compliance with laws and regulations, so you should ensure there is a program for compliance with state charitable solicitation requirements.

Reality Check (or How to Execute a Campaign)

I had just joined the board of my university alumni association and was attending my first meeting. A former board president and the development staff liaison presented a plan to raise funds to expand the alumni house. They wanted the board to indicate a goal that they felt could be raised from current and prior board members toward the cost of the expansion. After much discussion, a $2 million goal was agreed to, but that was considered a stretch since there had historically been no giving requirements for board members. At the next meeting a few months later, the vice president of advancement attended and shared that we were planning to start a major campaign. The first phase was to engage a consultant to build a case statement. Several of us were contacted by the consultant to share our thoughts on what the university meant to us and what emotional appeal would resonate best with contributors. Campaigns were relatively new in the history of the university, and the last campaign had raised less than $500 million. The consultants evaluated the capacity of the potential donors, provided their case statements, and suggested a goal of $600 million.

A bold campaign plan was developed. A campaign steering committee was formed that included both past significant supporters and younger potential supporters with high capacity for giving as well as the presidents of the affiliated foundation board, the alumni association board, and the annual giving board. The chair was wisely selected from the governing board of the university, who had also previously chaired the foundation board. The vice president of advancement (VPA) was new to his position and energetic, understood the culture of the university, and possessed a vision for building the team to make the campaign a success. The university president was excited about the prospect of the campaign and willing to provide the necessary focus to ensure success. The campaign steering committee boldly decided that the proposed goal was too low, that the campaign would be spread over nine years, and that a $1 billion was a more ambitious target. The VPA wisely suggested that campaign success should be defined by achieving three related goals—increasing alumni engagement, increasing the giving participation rate to 40% (which would put the university at the top of all public universities and among the top three of all national universities in giving participation by alumni), and raising $1 billion.

Financial investments were made in ramping up the staff for alumni engagement, development, and communications. Statistics were prepared as to the size and number of gifts needed to get to our goal. Goals by unit were set by their boards. Case statements by unit were written and the materials were printed. The materials reflected not the need as much as the emotional appeal. For example, it wasn't so much that the alumni house needed more room and updating but that alumni needed a welcoming home to come to, meet in, and even hold their wedding receptions in. Excitement built, and our alumni association board decided to substantially increase our commitment goal.

The silent phase was underway. Campaigns normally begin with a silent phase where they quietly approach major donors so they can launch publicly with more than 50% already pledged. Approximately three years into the campaign, a public launch occurred at homecoming, with staff, faculty, administration, and alumni sharing in the celebration. The celebration focused on the impact the campaign would have on the university and on each of our stakeholders. Regional celebrations were also planned for the next two years to build excitement around the country. Each focused on the impact the funds would have and, therefore, the impact the investment being made by our donors would have.

New alumni engagement activities were planned and executed, including taking the university on the road to areas where a critical mass of alumni lived. That weekend of unique experiences and access featured the best of our alumni as speakers or program leaders and brought the best of the university to our alumni, with faculty and deans leading sessions.

The importance of women as philanthropists was recognized with the formation of a women's leadership giving society. In addition to committing to the establishment of an endowment, they will focus on recruiting more women for leadership positions on boards and on campus. Finally, they will help celebrate the 100th anniversary of the admittance of women to the university with special programming. They met their goal of getting 100 women to pledge $10,000 for the endowment and are currently 50% over goal.

The participation goal of 40% is the most challenging with trends of declining participation across the country. This goal requires fostering a culture of giving at all age levels beginning with students. Impact week increases the visibility of the impact giving has on campus by featuring students who have benefited from scholarships, buildings built with donated funds, and faculty members supported by donor-endowed chairs. A day was established, called One Tribe One Day, which builds excitement around the world by getting everyone to give a gift on that day. With fun videos featuring the president, generous matching gifts for attaining certain levels of participation, competitions among schools and units, and events hosted by alumni around the world, we break previous participation records each year.

With two years left in the campaign, we have raised over 75% of our goal, and the funds are already having an impact. Many of our board members have caught the excitement and moved from ambassadors to advocates to askers. We even had a donor step forward with such enthusiasm for the alumni house expansion that we are expanding our expansion, breaking ground in a few months. We will raise our $1 billion.

CHAPTER FIVE

Investing for the Future

Unless you are a professional financial advisor, investor, or stockbroker, understanding the world of investing can be daunting. Just the language of *asset allocation*, *spending rate*, *hedge funds*, and *endowment model* can be overwhelming, and that is without defining all the various types of investments such as managed futures, derivatives, and options. Even if you are not a member of the investment or finance committee, you have a fiduciary responsibility as a board member to preserve the assets of the organization. Not every organization has an investment committee, and if one does not exist separately, the responsibility can be that of the finance committee.

Objectives of Investing

As discussed in Chapter 6, there are different types of financial assets with differing time frames for their investment. Endowments or permanently restricted funds have a longer-investing time frame because the principal is held in perpetuity and only the income spent. Unrestricted and temporarily restricted funds may have a shorter investing period since they may be spent for programs and operations. They should still be invested to maximize return, with only the portion needed in the very short term maintained as cash.

Generally, the investment objective is to emphasize long-term real growth based on a risk-adjusted total return approach. Have I lost you? *Long-term* is considered one complete investment cycle through up markets and down markets and historically is a 30-year span. *Real growth* refers to the growth in the portfolio that exceeds inflation plus any expenses. Therefore, if the portfolio value goes up 8% including interest, dividends, and realized and unrealized gains, but inflation is 4% and expenses are 2%, then the *real return* is 2% (8%–4%–2%). *Risk adjusted* represents the risk the organization is willing to take. This is up to the board and is primarily managed through asset diversification. *Total return* means that in evaluating the results of your investment strategy, you include interest, dividends, and realized and unrealized gains and losses net of expenses. It is not just the cash you receive from interest, dividends, and sales of the investments.

The board needs a road map, and for nonprofit organizations, the guiding map is the investment policy. The policy provides a framework to assist the board and should include guidelines for the selection of and monitoring of the organization's investments.

Outside Advisors

Most organizations seek the advice of an investment advisor or consultant. Selection of an investment advisor with expertise in handling the investments of a nonprofit with investments of a similar size is critical. Boards may think they have the expertise in-house with members who are professionals. However, engaging an investment advisor or consultant helps to ensure a breadth of investment experience across all types of investments and provides access to funds or investments that may not be otherwise available. The selection should be a result of a well-thought-out proposal process with oral presentations by two or three qualified firms. Investment managers who actually execute the investments may represent that they can serve as an advisor. However, there is an inherent conflict of interest here, since they will encourage investment in the funds or investments they manage. While there is an additional fee charged by the investment advisor based on the size of the portfolio, the fee is worth it if they provide advice and access that increases returns while reducing risk.

One decision the board must make is whether it wishes to give the advisor discretion or require the advisor to come back to the investment committee to approve each investment manager and/or investment. Given that the investment committee is composed of busy volunteer board members, requiring approval for every investment can increase risk. In the current fluctuating investment environment, a delay in a decision can be very costly. If discretion is given to the advisor, a discretionary agreement with the advisor must be drafted, which specifies what the advisor can and cannot do. Once the advisor is engaged, they can also assist in the drafting of the investment policy statement (IPS). The IPS is the guideline that the investment advisor must adhere to. The use of an investment advisor combined with a well-drafted IPS will also prevent investment bias from any individual board member.

Key Components of the Investment Policy Statement (see Sample Investment Policy Statement at the end of chapter)

- Objectives of the IPS—simple statements such as to develop a disciplined and systematic approach to investing in order to guide the committee in investment decision-making.

- Frequency of review—best practice is for the investment committee to review annually with modifications approved by the board.

- Roles and responsibilities of the board, the investment or finance committee, the investment advisor, and the investment managers need to be defined.

- Investment philosophy—identify specific investment asset classes that are permissible investments and state the percentage allocation ranges for each investment class. Such ranges can be specified as long-term goals with more specific ranges for a shorter time period such as the coming year.

- Prohibited investments may refer to types of investments or to individual companies, such as those that are not socially responsible. Organizations are finding that prohibiting investments in specific companies is difficult for investment managers because funds often invest in hundreds of companies. Also restrictions may be thematic and change over time. Board members should be sensitive that restrictions often have a negative impact on investment return, thereby reducing the funding available to support programs.

- Liquidity requirements—the organization needs to anticipate its cash flow needs and when it might require the investments to be sold or liquidated in order to have the funds for programmatic or operational needs. For instance, the policy may specify that all or a certain portion of the investments must be able to be liquidated within 90 days. This allows the investment advisor to ensure that that portion is not invested in illiquid assets.

- Performance benchmarks—each asset class has an investment industry benchmark to which the results of the investment fund can be compared. Since the goal of each investment manager should be to beat the benchmark, this is how their performance is evaluated. The decision to terminate a manager is often based on their long-term performance compared to the benchmark. For example, the results of domestic equities/stock managers who invest in large companies (known as large cap managers) are often compared to the S&P 500.

- Investment selection and monitoring—may specify the due diligence criteria the investment advisor should apply in recommending investments as well as any expense or fee guidelines. The IPS may also include the monitoring and performance reporting requirements of the investment advisor.

- Rebalancing—when the performance of a particular asset class is either very good or very poor, the asset class may be outside the asset allocation guidelines, and rebalancing of the portfolio may be required. The IPS may suggest the frequency and procedures for rebalancing of the portfolio.

Asset Allocation Strategy

The decisions related to asset allocation often have the greatest impact on the goal of maximizing return while minimizing risk. Without giving an economics lesson, and realizing that sometimes markets are irrational, different broad asset classes move in different directions. Equities generally move in a different direction from fixed income securities. Therefore, if the value of equities declines, the value of fixed income securities should increase. By diversifying your portfolio, you are reducing the risk of the value of every asset in the portfolio declining at the same time. Also, diversification within an asset class is critical. You do not want to invest in only one or a few companies or funds. Most policies specify a maximum threshold of 5%–10% within an asset class for any one company or mutual fund. Sometimes this can be a challenge if a large contribution of stock in one company is received from a donor who specifies the stock cannot be sold for a certain time.

New types of investments are being developed and offered regularly. Two guiding rules: If you do not understand the investment, do not invest in it. AND if it sounds too good to be true, it probably is.

Investments are categorized into equities, fixed income, alternatives/real assets, and cash equivalents.

Equities are further broken down:

- U.S. or domestic large, middle, and small capitalized companies (large, mid-, and small cap).
- International or global companies typically headquartered outside the United States, which are further broken down into developed markets (e.g., most European markets) and emerging markets (e.g., India or China).
- Equities may be held in funds that are classified as value versus growth. This means that the investment manager has made the decision to focus their investing on companies that are at a good price for their underlying economics (value) or on their potential to grow rapidly (growth).

Fixed income securities are composed of the following:

- Investment-grade bonds or corporate debt that have been rated above a certain level by the Moody's, Standard & Poor's, or other recognized rating agency. Some organizations state in their IPS that they will invest only in investment-grade securities in order to minimize risk since their ranking indicates a lower risk of the company defaulting on their debt.
- High-yield debt that provides a higher return but also a higher risk since there is a reason the company is borrowing at a higher rate of interest.
- These are also further categorized into domestic, globally developed, and emerging market companies.

- Tax-exempt fixed income securities are those that are issued through governments or related agencies that are exempt from taxes at either the federal, state, and/or local level. Because the rates are generally lower and nonprofit organizations generally do not pay taxes anyway, these are not typical investments for nonprofit organizations unless they are concerned about risk. These securities generally have a very low risk of decline in value.

Alternatives and real assets, which are generally less liquid than the aforementioned, include the following:

- Commodities such as gold or silver.
- Domestic and global real estate.
- Hedge funds that are mutual funds with specific purposes, generally designed for their value to move in the opposite direction of the general markets. While there has been publicity on rogue investment managers who have defrauded investors of certain hedge funds, and while hedge funds typically have higher expenses, well-researched and well-managed hedge funds are effective in reducing the risk of a portfolio. In times of market declines, having a hedge fund in your portfolio may reduce the losses experienced.
- Private equity that are funds or individual companies whose stock is not publicly traded on an exchange.
- Derivatives that include options and other securities that are tied to another underlying security.

Your investment advisor should be able to educate you thoroughly on these alternative investments and provide historical returns (which may not be indicative of future returns). This is an important category for investing both to maximize returns and to minimize risk, so do not be afraid of the alternatives and real assets category.

Cash equivalents include cash, certificates of deposit, and other short-term investments that generally have a maturity of 90 days or less. Yes, your asset allocation should include an allocation to this category even though the returns are minimal.

How much of your portfolio is allocated or invested in each of the above is up to the board, based on the funding needs of the organization, the level of risk the organization can take, and the spending policy.

Spending Policy

Nonprofit organizations always have more needs than funds. In order to ensure the future of the organization, the board must be disciplined in approving a budget that provides for the spending from the investments in a way that, over time, evens out unusual income and value swings. A best practice is to apply a spending rate each year. That spending rate is a percentage that factors in the expected investment total return, less expenses, less inflation. For example, if the expected long-term return is 8% and expenses are 2% and inflation is 1%, the spending rate should not be more than 5%. Another best practice is to apply that rate to the average of the last three years of the investment portfolio's total market value. This resolves the issue of unusual fluctuations in any one year. It is difficult to continue funding operations and programs consistently if in one year the market drops significantly, with the expectation it will recover, and you base your spending going forward on that one year. A decision that should also be included in the spending policy is how to factor major gifts into the computation. If a million-dollar gift is received near year-end, it will not have had a chance to earn any return, so it should not be included in the total market value of the investment portfolio for the calculation. Some organizations require a two- or three-year waiting period. The spending rate should be reviewed and approved annually in conjunction with the budget process.

Funds available for distribution should then be allocated to each unrestricted, temporarily restricted, and permanently restricted account on a pro rata basis. Often the method used to allocate the income is the unit value method whereby additions to such funds purchase units at the current market value, and the income is allocated based on the units the individual account holds. The staff performs this calculation, which can be complicated, so the purpose of this discussion is just to explain the terminology. The board needs to be comfortable that there is a fair, consistent, and accurate method to allocate funds available for spending. Occasionally a donor may request the value of the amount in, for example, the scholarship account they have set up. The organization needs to be able to provide the information. Each year, the amount that can be awarded for the scholarship in this example needs to be provided to the administrator for the account.

Reviewing the results of the investment portfolio and determining the proper spending rate are critical roles for the board member in executing their fiduciary responsibility.

Reality Check

Allison has just been appointed to the finance committee and immediately began asking questions relating to the sorority's $10 million of investments. Unfortunately, the committee member who was a stockbroker and the only one with any investment expertise has rotated off the committee. Because the stockbroker was the only one with any expertise, she was totally responsible for investing the entire portfolio. Her personal philosophy was an asset allocation of 60% in equities and 40% in fixed income. She had a couple of investment manager friends, so one handled the equities and the other fixed income. Allison had served on a much-larger foundation board that used an investment advisor/consultant. She was not comfortable with the prior situation and was concerned that the asset allocation both increased risk and did not maximize returns. At first, she suggested expanding the asset allocation to other categories, including hedge funds and international assets. She was met with a resounding "no way" from other members of the finance committee who had had confidence in the former stockbroker member. "We have never invested in such things, and my brother says he read about a hedge fund where everyone lost all their money while the manager got rich and hid his money in the Caymans."

Allison did not want the sole responsibility for making investment decisions and convinced the finance committee to form a subcommittee for investments that would add members with investment experience. Allison also realized the committee needed educating, and she proposed that an investment advisor be engaged. A proposal process ensued, with the potential consultants presenting how they provided access to funds the organization would not normally have access to, they would do the reporting the overworked finance director had previously had to prepare, their experience indicated that their fees would be offset by other savings as well as a higher total return, and they would help with the development of an investment policy once they learned more about the needs and risk profile. They would meet with the new investment subcommittee quarterly and the finance committee and board annually but would immediately reach out if there were more urgent issues in between.

An investment advisor was engaged and immediately began educating the committee and board on the different types of investments. Over the next few years, investment expertise was added to the investment subcommittee, a new investment policy was developed, and a spending policy was adopted. Preferring to reduce risk by investing in fund of funds for alternative investments, they did invest in hedge funds, real estate, and private equity funds. In 2008, when the equities markets declined significantly, the decision to expand into these types of investments saved them from losing a significant portion of their portfolio that would have resulted if they had stayed with their former philosophy. Of course, bringing on more investment expertise also meant bringing on more opinions. The expert in fixed income wanted to increase the allocation to fixed income, while the private equity expert wanted to go more to private equity. The investment advisor served as the unbiased voice of reason. When the decision was made to invest a small portion in commodities, getting the committee together to act quickly to approve a new investment manager or purchase a commodity fund became impractical. Volatility in that type of investment meant waiting 24 hours, which could result in a missed opportunity or a loss. Therefore, the investment advisor recommended, and the board approved giving the investment advisor discretion to execute transactions without the approval of the committee as long as they were within the investment policy guidelines. Trust has been built, with the board and finance committee comfortable that they are doing all they can to build the investment portfolio while minimizing risk, all of which means expanded programming and more scholarship awards.

SAMPLE INVESTMENT POLICY

1. Purpose of an Investment Policy Statement

The purpose of the Investment Policy Statement ("IPS") of the XYZ Organization is:

- To provide guidelines for the Investment Committee, the Board of Directors, and the investment consulting firm ("Consultant") to be more disciplined and systematic in decision making in order to understand and achieve the investment goals.
- To specify objectives and expectations so they are clarified for all concerned parties by providing a clear understanding between the Investment Committee ("the Committee"), and the Consultant with respect to the investment policy, guidelines and objectives of the portfolio as well as the limitations, and direction the Committee believes are most appropriate for this portfolio.
- To approve investment goals and the strategy to achieve the goals.
- To provide investment parameters such that investment decisions can be made under a variety of circumstances in a deliberate fashion, within documented, consistent guidelines.
- To provide an objective means to evaluate the performance of the Consultant and whether they are monitoring compliance with the IPS.
- To provide a means to communicate to Consultant, investment managers, and beneficiaries about how the Committee proposes to go about managing the investment portfolio.

2. Description

The primary purpose for the Investment Portfolio is to assist, support, and foster the mission of XYZ Organization by maintaining and growing principal, by being prudent in establishing the annual payout, and providing a hedge against inflation. The Board of Directors (the "Board") has elected to have at a minimum __% of its funds invested in socially responsible investments, as more fully described below.

3. Tax Status

The XYZ Organization ("the Organization") is a tax-exempt, private, not-for-profit corporation, as defined in Section 501(c)(3) of the Internal Revenue Code so is generally not required to pay taxes on its investment income as long as it expends such income for its tax-exempt purposes. Management and the Board will consult with its audit and tax firm for advice related to the taxability of such income.

4. Investment Administration

The Committee is a sub-committee of the Finance Committee. Any changes to this document must be presented to the Finance Committee and in turn the Board for approval. The Committee need not approve changes in specific managers of the investment portfolio provided the changes are within the guidelines set forth in this Investment Policy Statement.

5. Investment Objectives

The Committee establishes and can revise periodically the overall direction of the investment portfolio. Currently, the investment direction is to provide real, long term growth based upon a risk adjusted total return approach to managing the portfolio, consistent with the risk parameters and guidelines established by the Committee. The Committee has no expected immediate need for the portfolio assets and is willing to accept short-term volatility in order to achieve higher expected rates of return over the long run.

As previously mentioned, the Committee has agreed to abide by the following guidelines for socially responsible investing:

Companies that support or produce the following are considered prohibited investments:

- Racial Discrimination
- Gender Discrimination
- Pornography
- Production and Sale of Weapons
- Antipersonnel Landmines
- Poor Labor Standards/Sweatshop

The Organizations investments will have at least __% of its assets invested in companies that abide by the guidelines listed above. It is understood that while individual managers may fall below __%, the entire portfolio must meet the __% threshold.

Due to the requirements of __% of the investment portfolio must be invested in managers that meet social responsibility guidelines; there is a much smaller universe of acceptable managers and funds to choose from. As a result of this limited universe, there is a high probability that the returns of the portfolio will be less than that of a portfolio without such restrictions.

Consultant typically requires a three-year track record before recommending an investment manager; however, because of the resulting smaller universe, Consultant may invest in managers who have a track record of 18 months provided it has the approval of the Committee. The Committee reserves the right to grant exceptions to this minimum requirement.

Liquidity and Income Needs

Currently, XYZ Organization does not depend on the assets of the investment portfolio to meet its operating needs. However, the Board has approved a spending rate policy of not more than __% of the average net asset market value of the most recent trailing 12 quarters that may be withdrawn.

Time Horizon

For the purpose of planning, the time horizon for the investment portfolio is 7–10 years. Capital values do fluctuate, and the Committee recognizes that the possibility of capital loss does exist. Historical asset class return data suggest that the shorter the holding period, the greater the risk of the objectives not being achieved.

6. Responsibilities of _____ as Investment Consultant

XYZ Organization has engaged Consultant to provide advice concerning the management of the investment portfolio. Advice will be consistent with the investment objectives and guidelines set forth in this Investment Policy Statement.

Consultant's general responsibilities will be the following:

- Assist in the development and periodic review of strategic investment policy, including asset allocation.
- Conduct Investment Manager searches including performing due diligence on each manager.
- Provide ongoing due diligence and research on Investment Managers, asset classes, and economic market trends.
- Rebalance the asset allocation as necessary.
- Monitor the performance of the Investment Manager(s) to determine whether the Investment Managers are complying with stated investment objectives.

Consultant will have general discretion within the parameters of the aforementioned items and specific investment discretion and authority to make decisions relating to selection of investment managers and the amounts to invest with each manager provided the actions are within the guidelines of the asset allocation defined in this document.

7. Asset Allocation

The Committee in consultation with Consultant has established the following diversified asset allocation strategy to achieve the investment goals and objectives on a positive risk adjusted basis of the investment portfolio. Asset classes may be added or deleted depending upon their fundamental allocation subject to approval by the Committee and the Board. Rebalancing should be considered if any asset class approaches or exceeds either the recommended low or high end of its range. In any event, rebalancing will be accomplished at least annually.

ASSET ALLOCATION

Asset Class	Low	Target	High
Domestic Equities	30%	45%	65%
International Equities	5%	20%	30%
Alternative Investments	0%	5%	25%
Fixed Income/Credit	5%	15%	30%
Real Assets	5%	15%	25%
Cash & Cash Equivalents	0%	0%	10%

The approved asset allocation set out above indicates an initial target allocation for each asset class. From time to time, based on changing economic circumstances or new academic research, it may be desirable to make changes in the target allocation. The Committee must present to the Finance Committee and the Board any proposed changes in the form of a written amendment to this Investment Policy Statement for approval.

In some market conditions it may be necessary to increase the portfolio's allocation to cash as a tactical or strategic move in severe market conditions. If these changes would result in the asset allocation outside of the approved ranges, the changes will not be made without the expressed written or verbal consent of the Committee.

Not more than 10% of the total assets may be invested in a single-manager's investment strategy and no manager having multiple strategies in the portfolio shall exceed more than 20% of the total investment assets. No one underlying position in a single company shall exceed more than 5% of the total investment assets.

With the exception of U.S. Government/Agency securities or cash equivalents, not more than 10% of any manager's portfolio, at market value, may be invested in the securities of one issuer.

The traditional fixed income portfolio should maintain, in aggregate, an investment grade credit rating of AA-/Aa3 or higher. Investments in international fixed income and domestic high yield securities with a credit rating of B or higher are permitted so long as they do not exceed 20% of the traditional fixed income portfolio.

Alternative Investments may include hedge funds, which are mutual funds with specific purposes, generally designed for their value to move in the opposite direction of the general markets. Hedge funds must be well researched and managed and have a goal of reducing the risk in the portfolio.

Real Assets permitted may include commodities and real estate including domestic and international real estate mutual funds or investment trusts.

8. Monitoring, Reporting and Revisions

The investment portfolio will be monitored, and performance will be measured in the following manner:

- Monthly performance of the investment portfolio will be reported in time-weighted and dollar-weighted format. This monthly report will be a summary of the overall portfolio.

- Quarterly performance of the investment portfolio will be reported in a time-weighted and dollar-weighted format as an overview of how the portfolio has performed as well as detailed analytics of each underlying manager.

- A comprehensive review of investment returns by manager will be presented to the Committee on a quarterly basis, or more often, if deemed necessary by the Committee.

Consultant will furnish quarterly reports regarding:

- Adherence of investment managers to the guidelines expressed in this Investment Policy Statement.

- Material changes in an investment manager's organization, investment philosophy, investment or trading processes or personnel.

- Comparisons of each investment manager's investment results to appropriate indices as defined in the Investment Policy Statement.

- The investment returns will be compared against the following benchmarks:

  - A total weighted index based upon the weighted average of asset classes in the portfolio.

- Investment managers within the portfolio will be compared to individual benchmarks based upon the specific asset class of that manager.

- The Standard & Poor's 500 Index

- Blended index of 70% MSCI ACWI Index and 30% Barclays Capital U.S. Aggregate Index

As previously mentioned, as a result of a limited universe, there is a high probability that the returns of the portfolio will be less than that of a portfolio without social responsibility restrictions. Consultant will continue to actively monitor those managers that are in the universe to continually measure their respective performance relative to the universe.

Revisions

This Investment Policy Statement should be reviewed annually for necessary modifications resulting from changes in the organization's liquidity requirements as well as investment market circumstances. This Investment Policy Statement shall remain in effect until revised or amended by the Committee.

Approved:

_____   _____

(Date)   (Signature, Board Secretary)

_____   _____

(Date)   (Signature, Finance Committee Chair)

_____   _____

(Date)   (Signature, Investment Committee Chair)

We accept this investment plan and the investment objectives within the guidelines given.

_____   _____

(Date)   (Signature, Consultant Representative)

(Developed by Palmer P. Garson, investment professional and member of numerous nonprofit organization boards and investment committees.) The above is an example for an organization with a restrictive socially responsible mandate. Many organizations may elect to eliminate those restrictions and/or have others.

CHAPTER SIX

Understanding the Financial Statements and Tax Reporting Requirements

One of the key fiduciary responsibilities of a board member is monitoring the financial status of the organization. While the finance committee normally focuses on this responsibility, every board member should be able to understand the financial statements presented at each meeting. Best practice for financial reporting should be the presentation of internal financial statements at least quarterly compared to the budget and the prior year.

The format for these internal financial statements should coincide with the budget format and should be customized to meet the priorities of the organization. The level of detail is up to the finance committee but should be at a sufficient level so that the board understands the results of key activities or events and can determine that there is adequate liquidity (cash or assets available to be converted to cash) to meet the operating and programmatic needs of the organization for the next year.

The board must also be able to assess the financial management skills of the organization's management and confirm that any restrictions imposed by donors or granting organizations are being complied with. Finally, the board is responsible for ensuring that adequate financial controls are in place to minimize the risk of fraud or misstatement of the financial reports.

It sounds pretty daunting—especially since nonprofit financial reporting is spoken in a different language than what you may be accustomed to in the for-profit business world. And nonprofits never have enough staff, so how can they be assured the financial controls are adequate?

Financial Controls

Internal financial controls consist of all the policies and procedures an organization puts in place to ensure orderly and efficient conduct of its activities, safeguarding of its assets, prevention and detection of fraud and errors, accuracy and completeness of the accounting records, and timely preparation of reliable financial information. The framework of a good internal control system includes the following:

- A sound control environment created by management through communication, attitude, and example. This includes a focus on integrity, a commitment to investigating discrepancies, diligence in designing systems, and assigning responsibilities.
- A risk assessment identifying the areas in which the greatest threat or risk of inaccuracies or loss exists.
- Monitoring and reviewing the system of internal control periodically to ensure that internal control activities have not become obsolete or lost due to turnover or other factors.
- Control activities that are critical policies and procedures that require authorization for transactions and activities and documentation of all transactions. They include the reconciliation of financial assets such as cash to bank or investment statements. They also include asset security, both physical and electronic, controls to prevent unauthorized access or theft.

The control issue where many nonprofits may be weak, due to low staffing levels, is segregation of duties. No staff member or volunteer with access to assets, such as those who receive cash or checks, should have the ability to perform record-keeping or reconciliation procedures. They could then misappropriate the funds and cover their actions by changing the records. Compensating controls need to be established. The organization's chief executive, who normally would not perform any record-keeping, may need to review the bank reconciliation, manually sign all checks, and/or issue all donor correspondence. The treasurer or board chair should approve all material disbursements and contracts.

As a board member, you are also part of the control activities as you review the financial results in comparison with budget. Unusual trends in revenues and expenses and variances from budget all require investigation because they may indicate fraud or error. Taking the time to understand the organization's financials and budget, asking questions, and insisting that financial results are reported in a timely manner are all part of a board member's responsibilities.

Budgeting

The annual operating and capital budget is one of the most effective tools to establish organization priorities and provide financial control. The board's role in budget development begins with the strategic plan. Once the plan is finalized, the goals for the year and the related resource needs to achieve those goals should be the starting point for the budget development. Many organizations merely take the prior year forecasted results and increase them by a percentage. Instead, a fresh look should be taken each year to ensure progress toward goals.

Since a nonprofit organization raises funds and generates revenues solely to fund expenses to fulfill its mission, its budget should generally reflect revenues equal to expenses, known as a balanced budget. Nonprofit organizations do not exist to accumulate wealth, but they may decide to reserve or put aside funds for a future program or capital expense. Because they often do not have excess cash flow, a prudent decision may be made by the board to maintain reserves to fund activities and commitments that occur prior to the generation of revenue. For example, a university may plan homecoming activities that require deposits and other cash outlays prior to the receipt of event revenues. Thus, a cash flow forecast should be developed in addition to a budget.

Once the revenues are budgeted, expenses must be limited to total revenues. Expense budgets must be realistic since they will be the guideline for disbursements for the year. Given the goals and priorities established, what is the best, efficient use of the limited resources? Often compensation and benefits represent the largest portion of the expenses for a nonprofit. Changes in compensation and benefits should be driven by the personnel evaluation process. Be sure the executive director has funds to reward those who were the strongest performers. Also remember to fairly compensate the executive director. What programmatic changes are planned for the coming year? What will be the staffing and other resource impact of those changes? Always ask if the changes are consistent with the priorities of the strategic plan.

A capital expense budget should also be prepared, ideally for the next three years since it will often be necessary to accumulate or borrow the funds for the capital projects over the longer term. It is also the responsibility of the board to ensure that plans are executed to lease, build, maintain, refurbish, and/or grow facilities as necessary to execute the mission of the organization.

The typical budget review process is shown in Figure 6.1.

Figure 6.1

Internal Financial Reporting

Financial reporting for management and the board should occur monthly, with reports issued to the finance committee and/or board. For internal reporting, a more detailed and programmatic financial presentation, consistent with how the organization budgets, may better meet the needs of the organization. The allocation of shared costs will be discussed further under external reporting. Utilizing accrual accounting, which is consistent with external reporting. is recommended, but some small organizations may maintain their internal records on a cash basis. Accrual accounting recognizes liabilities or amounts due to others and receivables such as pledges when they are incurred or received and provides a more complete picture of the financial position of the organization.

Table 6.1 is a simple example of an internal financial statement that breaks out revenues and expenses by program or functional area.

What concerns should you have about the following internal financial statement? You might ask why seminar revenue was less than budget or how it compared to the prior year. You might ask why administration costs are running more than budget and what they are forecasted to be for the remainder of the year.

Table 6.1

Sample Internal Financial Report

	Second Quarter			Year to Date		
Revenue	Budget	Actual	Variance	Budget	Actual	Variance
Program A	$200	$210	$ 10	$ 200	$ 210	$ 10
Seminars	50	40	(10)	100	90	(10)
Gifts	500	600	100	1,200	1,400	200
Total	$750	$850	$100	$1,500	$1,700	$200
Expenditures						
Administration	$100	$105	($5)	$ 200	$ 210	($10)
Seminars	100	80	20	200	160	40
Development	100	100	0	200	200	0
Program A	450	400	50	900	850	50
Total	$750	$685	$ 65	$1,500	$1,420	$ 80
Excess	$ 0	$165	$165	$ 0	$ 280	$280

External Financial Reporting

Generally accepted accounting principles specify the accounting requirements, and the Financial Accounting Standards Board (FASB) specifies the requirements for external reporting. Annually, the organization will issue financial statements, ideally having them audited by a public accounting firm. A new board member may find them confusing since they look different than other for-profit financial statements they may have seen in the past. They should look different since nonprofits' revenues consist of contributed resources and operate to pursue a public mission rather than to make a profit. A nonprofit's stakeholders include donors, lenders, grantors, members, beneficiaries, and volunteers, even the public in some cases, none of whom have ownership interests. The nonprofit's financial statements are generated to provide financial information for those who are considering lending, volunteering, granting funds, or donating to the nonprofit.

On August 18, 2016, the FASB issued a new standard on nonprofit reporting that updated the former reporting standard, known as Financial Accounting Standard No. 117, which had been in use since 1993. The goal according to FASB was to simplify the face of the financial statements and improve the usefulness of disclosures about the resources and the changes in those resources. Because the effective date is for annual financial statements issued for fiscal years beginning after December 15, 2017, and because early application is permitted, this chapter will discuss the new standard.

Comparison of For-Profit and Not-for-Profit Financial Statements

It may seem like a foreign language. Table 6.2 compares for-profit financial statements to not-for-profit financial statements. The first key term you should understand follows:

- Net assets—the excess or deficiency of assets over liabilities. Net assets are divided into two (formerly three) mutually exclusive classes based on the existence or absence of donor-imposed restrictions.

Table 6.2

Corporate For-Profit	Not-for-Profit
Balance sheet	Statement of financial position
Changes in shareholders' equity	Changes in net assets
Income statement	Statement of activities
Statement of cash flows	Statement of cash flows

- Net assets with donor restrictions—may include grants restricted for a purpose or with a time restriction (e.g., required to be held for X years). Either on the face of the statement of financial position or in the notes to the financial statements, a nonprofit should segregate those

  - maintained in perpetuity or
  - expected to be spent over time and/or
  - restricted for a specific purpose

- Net assets without donor restrictions:

  - Board designated—those net assets the board designates to be used for a particular purpose, such as a liquidity reserve or special program. The board may also designate that only the earnings on the designated amount can be expended for a particular purpose. The board may reverse its designation at any time.

- The former standard required that those with donor restrictions be further broken into those temporarily versus permanently restricted, but the new standard does not make this distinction.

Therefore, what should you look for on the statement of financial position? The assets are listed in the order of their liquidity and may or may not be classified into current or noncurrent assets. Unique assets to consider are as follows:

- Contributions or pledges receivable—donations or written commitments to make a donation in the future that may require a reserve for uncollectible amounts. Contributions due in more than one year will be discounted to reflect the time value of their receipt.

- Investments—may be significant and will be segregated into short-term and long-term investments. Any assets restricted to investment in land, buildings, and equipment also need to be separated on the statement.

- Assets held in trust by others—are held outside the organization, but any earnings and possibly ultimately the underlying assets are paid to the benefit of the organization.

Liabilities unique to nonprofit organizations include the following:

- Annuity trust obligations resulting from split interest agreements—executed between the organization and a donor and come in many variations. A simple example of a split interest agreement is one in which a donor contributes an amount to an organization with the provision that the organization will make an annuity payment to the donor or their beneficiary for a set time period or for the remainder of their life. The organization records the assets

Table 6.3

Sample Statement of Financial Position

Assets:	2018	2017
Cash & cash equivalents	$ 200	$ 250
Accounts receivable	50	45
Contributions receivable	300	250
Investments	600	550
Property & equipment, net	400	405
Total assets	$ 1,550	$ 1,500
Liabilities and net assets:		
Accounts payable	$ 130	$ 100
Unearned revenue	80	100
Annuity trust obligations	90	100
Long-term debt	150	160
Total liabilities	$ 450	$ 460
Net assets:		
Without donor restrictions	900	850
With donor restrictions	200	190
Total net assets	1,100	1,040
Total liabilities & net assets	$ 1,550	$ 1,500

(Based on FASB Accounting Standards Update 2016–14 Implementation Guidance and Illustrations)

received and a liability based on actuarial computations for the annuity due the donor with the difference reflected as contribution revenue.

- Deferred or unearned revenues—if an organization charges program fees or receives membership dues in advance of the event or period covered, they should be recognized as unearned or deferred revenue.

Table 6.3 is a simple example of a statement of financial position.

Statements of Activities and Changes in Net Assets

The statement of activities reports changes in the net assets segregating those with and without donor restrictions, either in one column beginning with the changes in net assets without donor restrictions followed by the changes in net assets with donor restrictions or in two columns, one for each of the classes. Revenues and gains typically include contributions, program fees, gain on sale of fixed assets, and investment return, net. Investment returns are required to be presented net of all expenses whether they are incurred externally or internally such as by an organization's own investment management staff.

A unique concept of nonprofit financial reporting relates to the release of net assets from restrictions. Remember that contributions restricted by the donor for a particular purpose or time period are recorded in the net assets with donor restrictions. However, all expenses are recorded under net assets without donor restrictions. Therefore, when the purpose or time restriction is met, a reduction in the net assets with donor restrictions occurs, and an increase in net assets (revenues) without donor restrictions is recorded. For example, if a donor restricts their contribution for an educational program, the contribution will be recognized in the "with donor restrictions" column on the statement of activities. When the expenses for the educational program occur and are recognized in the "without donor restrictions" column, a new line item entitled "net assets released from restrictions, satisfaction of program restrictions" is included, with a negative amount under the "with donor restrictions" column and the same, but positive, amount listed under the "without donor restrictions" column. Both are normally listed under revenues, gains, and other support.

Expenses and losses unique to nonprofit organizations include a functional listing by program (education conference, scholarship, research grant, etc.), management and general, membership development, and fund-raising. Additionally, in one place, on the face of the statement, as a separate statement of functional expenses, or in notes to the financial statements, the amounts of expenses by both their natural classification and their functional classification are required. Examples of natural expense classifications are salaries and wages, employee benefits, professional services, interest, depreciation, and rent. FASB lists functional expenses as program services and supporting activities with management and general supporting activities being those not directly identifiable with a program, fund-raising, or membership development activities. When preparing a statement of functional expenses, it is important to evaluate and understand how shared expenses, such as rent, are allocated across the activities. Examples of nonprofit losses are losses on the disposal of fixed assets and the actuarial loss on annuity trust obligations. Table 6.4 is a simple example of a statement of activities and changes in net assets excluding expenses by natural classification.

Statement of Cash Flows

The statement of cash flows also has some unique characteristics for non-profits. Operating and investing activities are pretty straightforward and consistent with the for-profit world. Financing activities include proceeds from

Table 6.4

Sample Statement of Activities and Changes in Net Assets

For the Year Ended
December 31, 2018

	Without Donor Restrictions	With Donor Restrictions	Total
Revenue, gains & other support			
Program fees	$ 120	$ —	$ 120
Membership dues	440		440
Contributions	600	600	1,200
Investment return, net	100	20	120
Net assets released from restrictions	600	(600)	—
Total revenue, gains & other support	$1,860	$ 20	$ 1,880
Expenses & losses			
Program A	$1,300		$ 1,300
Seminar program	100		100
Total program services	1,400		1,400
Administration	200		200
Development	200		200
Total expenses	1,800	—	1,800
Loss on sale of equipment	10		10
Actuarial loss on annuity trust obligations		10	10
Total expenses and losses	$1,810	$ 10	$ 1,820
Change in net assets	50	10	60
Net assets beginning of year	850	190	1,040
Net assets end of year	$ 900	$ 200	$ 1,100

(Based on FASB Accounting Standards Update 2016–14 Implementation Guidance and Illustrations)

contributions restricted for endowments and those subject to annuity trust agreements. Other financing activities include investment income restricted by a donor for reinvestment and payments of annuity obligations. Noncash activities required to be disclosed as supplemental data on the statement are noncash gifts such as equipment and paid-up life insurance policies.

Notes to Financial Statements

The notes to the financial statements are meant to clarify what is presented in the financial statements and are an integral part of the financial statements. The disclosures in the notes are prescribed by FASB. Typical notes for a not-for-profit include the following:

- Summary of accounting policies beginning with an explanation of the mission or purpose and legal structure of the organization. Here is the opportunity to describe for potential donors the organization in a concise fashion.
- Other accounting policies consistent with all generally accepted accounting policies (GAAP) disclosure requirements. Often nonprofits have relationships with other entities such as the university they support or other nonprofits they make grants to. Those relationships and the amounts of transactions are required to be disclosed in a note to the financial statements.
- Amounts and purposes of board designations that result in self-imposed restrictions on the use of resources as of the end of the period.
- Composition of donor-imposed restrictions and how those restrictions affect the availability of resources. The example provided by FASB in the implementation guidance of the new standard lists the composition of net assets with donor restrictions by the amount subject to expenditure for a specified purpose by program, the amount subject to passage of time, the amount subject to spending policy and appropriation, the amount subject to appropriation and expenditure when a specified event occurs, and any amounts not subject to appropriation or expenditure, such as a fixed asset or land that is required to be used for a certain purpose.
- Liquidity—a discussion of the organization's ability to manage liquidity and meet its cash flow needs for the next 12 months. FASB provides an illustration of liquidity disclosure that begins with total financial assets (excluding inventory and long-term investments) and deducts those assets unavailable for general expenditures within one year due to restrictions or board designations to arrive at those financial assets available to meet the general cash needs within one year. Disclosure of any borrowing arrangements to help meet liquidity needs is also required. For example, the following might be included in a footnote titled "Liquidity and Availability of Resources":

For purposes of analyzing resources available to meet general expenditures for 2020, XYZ Organization considers financial assets that will be collected and available for 2020 programs that are ongoing to the Organization. The Organization's investments are readily convertible to cash if it was to need additional liquidity. Financial assets available within one year are as follows:

Cash and cash equivalents	$ 1,000
Investments	10,000
Receivables	500
Financial assets available to meet cash needs for general expenditure within one year	$11,500

- Investments and the organization's spending policy include the investment policies with the return objectives and risk parameters and the strategies for achieving the return objectives.
- Common financial indicators are often quoted to assist in evaluating the effectiveness of the financial management of an organization:
    - Program spending ratio—computed by dividing total program expenses by total expenses.
    - Fund-raising efficiency ratio—computed by dividing fund-raising expenses by total funds raised (contributions).
    - Proper cost allocation is critical. The methods used to allocate costs between programs and support functions such as fund-raising must be disclosed. Historically, there has been great inconsistency related to cost allocation, so FASB is hoping that disclosure of the methods will improve transparency and consistency. Board members should have an understanding of the methodology for cost allocation. For example, occupancy costs may be allocated based on square footage occupied by each functional area, while salaries and benefits may be allocated based on estimates of time devoted to a program or administrative function.

Endowment Fund

Another financial term you will need to understand is "endowment fund." A donor (or the board may designate) makes a contribution stating that the assets must be invested by the organization for a set period or in perpetuity with only the income available to be used for either restricted or unrestricted purposes. As discussed in the chapter on investing, most organizations establish a spending policy that provides for a rate that over time will approximate the total return of the investments, net of expenses. Endowment funds are generally established to provide a source of income for the nonprofit.

As discussed in the chapter on investing, laws and regulations as to the spending of net appreciation of donor-restricted endowment funds vary by jurisdiction; however, most states have adopted some form of the Uniform Prudent Management of Institutional Funds Act of 2006 as guidance for nonprofits. As a board member, it is important to understand the organization's policy related to the spending of net appreciation. The appropriation from donor endowment in accordance with the spending policy and donor restrictions is an example of net assets released from restrictions. At times, the value of an endowment fund may decline below the amount originally donated and required to be invested for a long time or for perpetuity. These are referred to as "underwater endowment funds." These most often occur during a market decline shortly after the contribution is made. The amount and effects of underwater endowment funds, including the nonprofit's ability to spend from such funds, are now a required disclosure.

Also required is a reconciliation of the beginning and ending balance of the endowment(s) in total and by net asset class, including contributions, investment return, and amounts appropriated under the spending policy for unrestricted purposes.

Before you panic, you are not expected to be an expert in annual financial reporting. The organization's auditors are the experts and can answer questions. This information is merely to assist you when you are presented with the annual financial statements.

Financial Statement Audit, Review, or Compilation

As a board member, you are responsible for engaging the outside professional audit firm.

There are alternative levels of services provided by public accounting firms, with an audit being the highest level of service and preferable since it provides the highest level of assurance. At the conclusion of their audit, an opinion is issued as to whether the financial statements present fairly, in all material respects, the financial position, changes in net assets, and cash flows for the year in accordance with generally accepted accounting principles. If there are no exceptions to this opinion, it is considered a clean or unmodified report. The opinion letter is the first page of the audited financial statements and should be the first page reviewed by the board. The audit firm is also required to provide certain required communications to the board and/or its finance committee, including

- significant accounting policies,
- planned scope and timing of the audit,
- audit adjustments,

- difficulties encountered,
- management judgments and estimates,
- any management advisory services performed by the firm,
- issues discussed prior to retention,
- consultation with other accountants,
- management representations,
- any material weaknesses in internal controls as well as significant deficiencies.

Other control or efficiency improvement recommendations identified during the audit may be communicated only to management. Board members should ask if there were any such recommendations communicated only to management.

The evaluation and selection of an audit firm is normally conducted by the finance committee after reviewing responses to requests for proposal. The finance committee then presents its recommendation for audit firm to the full board for discussion and approval.

Another level of service is a compilation for organizations that need help in preparing their financial statements. A review, on the other hand, may be adequate for entities that must report their financial positions to third parties, such as creditors or regulatory agencies. A review requires that the firm performing it be independent and have an understanding of the organization and the nonprofit industry, with procedures performed generally limited to inquiry and analytical analysis. While fees are lower for these services, a good audit firm will add value during the audit that more than covers the increased fees.

Tax and Other Compliance Reporting

Nonprofit organizations are required to file with the Internal Revenue Service (IRS) for tax-exempt status. Once they have received their notice of exemption from taxation, they still are required to file an annual return. The specific form an organization must file depends on the level of gross receipts and the amount of its total assets as shown in Table 6.5.

Your audit firm or tax advisor normally prepares the 990 using information provided by management and the financial statements. However, the board has a responsibility to review the form prior to filing. Also, because these forms are a matter of public record and used by charity rating organizations, it is critical that the board and management thoroughly review the forms and consider that information can be extracted from them and posted online. How your mission and purpose are listed on the return and the costs classified becomes the basis for the ratings, and therefore, you should consider how best to portray your organization. Form 990 includes several

Table 6.5

Gross Receipts	Total Assets	Form Filed
<$50,000		990-N via E-postcard
<$200,000	<$500,000	990-EZ
Above those amounts		990
Private foundation		990PF

(www.irs.gov/charities-non-profits/form-990-series-which-forms-do-exempt-organizations-file-filing-phase-in)

questions that let the public know how well your organization manages its fiscal responsibility through its policies and board oversight. For certain organizations such as hospitals, audited financial statements are required by the 990 instructions. Even if not required, it is a good idea to complete the audit prior to submission of the 990.

In addition, if the organization receives revenues from nonexempt activities, as defined by the IRS, it may be required to pay unrelated business income taxes. Again, board members are not expected to be tax experts; however, they should know enough to ask questions as to whether the organization incurred any such taxable income. For certain nonprofits, the board will be required to adopt annually a statement committing that any excess funds will be carried over to the following year to be used for educational and charitable purposes in accordance with the tax-exempt mission of the organization. There also are tests that foundations and public charities must comply with to maintain their charitable, tax-exempt status. These are built into their applicable tax filing.

One confusing point for some is that just because an organization is exempt from income taxes does not mean it is exempt from state sales taxes. Each state has different requirements for granting sales tax exemption. As a board member, ask the staff to investigate those guidelines.

Depending on the nature of any grants received from governmental entities, there may be extensive compliance requirements and reporting required. As a board member, inquire as to the nature of these compliance requirements. Federal grant reporting requirements are extensive. If they are not significant to the organization, you may ask if the compliance requirements are worth the funding received.

The required annual registration and reporting for states where the organization solicits funds normally includes attaching the 990 and the audited financial statements. As a board member, inquire as to whether the organization is required to register and provide annual reporting to states. The states can assess significant penalties if an organization solicits without registering.

Transparency

Transparency by an organization, in its annual financial reports, tax reporting, or other compliance reporting, is increasingly important. Many organizations issue an annual report providing not only summary financial information but also the accomplishments of the organization during the year. Often the report is used to thank donors and make them aware of all their gifts have accomplished.

You never want anything to occur that would cause embarrassment to the organization or its board and negatively impact the ability to attract resources. Nonprofits and their boards should hold themselves to the highest level of integrity. Boards must be vigilant in their oversight responsibilities. There may be transactions that, while not material to the organization, should still be approved by the board or one of its committees. One of these is the compensation of the executive(s) of the organization, which is disclosed on the 990 if over a certain amount. A few years ago, excessive compensation received by the executive director of an organization brought negative press and impacted the organization significantly for years. Be alert for these types of transactions and ask questions.

Use your common sense and maintain an attitude that the organization's assets should be managed as prudently as you manage your own personal assets. As a board member, you are serving not only the organization but also the public it benefits.

Reality Check

The Society of XYZ is a well-respected organization of executives with an interest in promoting international business. In addition to holding annual programs providing education and networking opportunities for its members, it conducts educational programming for entrepreneurs—the next generation of business leaders around the world—as well as international travel programs. As a rapidly growing organization, its financial systems and controls had not kept up with its growth in programming. The executive director also maintained the financial records without any formal accounting training. All transactions were entered via financial software that did not provide fund accounting capabilities. Programs were rapidly expanding with the support of key member sponsors that devoted their time, talent, and treasure to creating and executing the programs. The organization got more complicated with programs and affiliated boards around the world. The executive director increasingly had to spend more of her time on maintaining the financial records and less on programs, membership growth, and staff supervision and development.

The board received regular consolidated financial reports and information on the various programs. Annually, a consolidated budget was presented and approved by the board, but the most recent one reflected an overall loss. The internal financial statements went on for several pages but did not provide the information needed to identify financial problems. A few board members became concerned that the profitability of individual programs was not being analyzed properly and that losses were being offset by the profitability of other programs. A financial sustainability task force began evaluating the future of the organization. How costs should be allocated became a subject of debate.

As a new member of the society with nonprofit financial expertise, the treasurer of the board approached me to get involved. The executive director was open to meeting with me and explaining the complexities of the organization. She had historically relied on her audit firm to assist her with financial reporting and had recently hired a bookkeeper to assist with collections and disbursements. It quickly became apparent that the audit firm had not taken the time to understand the complexities of the organization. Also, there was no finance, audit, or investment committee to support the executive director and review the financial information. Here was an organization of business executives frustrated by the lack of the information needed to ensure that the mission of the organization was being efficiently carried out.

Most important, the internal financial statement format and chart of accounts did not reflect information consistent with the programmatic priorities of the society. The board could not evaluate the financial results of the programs. Once I gained an understanding of the society's activities and met with the audit firm, I outlined a new financial reporting format that extracted the data from the financial software in a program-by-program format. This required that all transactions be entered not only by natural expense account such as salaries and wages but also by functional class, which included every program or administrative function. Suddenly the board had the financial report it needed to evaluate the financial status of each of the society's programs. The staff estimated the time they devoted to each program or administrative function so that the full direct and indirect costs could be considered. While not perfect, it was a simple, quick solution to getting the board the information they needed.

Other best practices outlined in this chapter are being implemented, including the creation of a finance, audit, and investment committee. Transparency and communication have improved. When organizations grow rapidly and are blessed with growing resources to expand programming, sometimes the systems and control procedures do not keep up with the growth. Luckily, in this situation the board identified the risk and dealt with it before the situation became critical.

CHAPTER SEVEN

Planning for the Future

Chances are sometime during your first year someone will say, "We need to schedule our strategic planning session." Hopefully your board is annually taking a fresh perspective on planning for the future or at least updating the plan developed in the past couple of years. Change is happening quickly in today's world, and organizations need to adjust as quickly.

There is no precise methodology or "right way" to conduct strategic planning. What is important is that strategic discussions occur among strategic thinkers. Not everyone is a strategic thinker. In a recent discussion at the Governmental Affairs Conference of the Credit Union National Association, former president George W. Bush talked about Russia's president Vladimir Putin. Specifically, he indicated that Putin was not a strategic thinker. President Bush defined a strategic thinker as one who focuses discussions on how we can win together. He said Putin focuses on how he can make you lose. While you may not have Putin in the room, you may have staff or board members with their favorite programs that they want to prioritize.

Planning for Planning

So how do you get everyone excited and focused as strategic thinkers for a strategic planning session? The preparation for the session is critical. Sufficient time must be set aside and not just a few hours in the middle of a board meeting. It may not be possible to accomplish everything in one session. These sessions can be emotionally charged and therefore exhausting. Sometimes it may be important to hit the pause button and get back together later. You may need to gather more data.

The environment should be conducive to strategic thinking. Consider a new location that provides plenty of space for subgroup breakout sessions.

To get participants to think "out of the box," they need to be outside their normal meeting space. For example, The College of William & Mary Mason School of Business has a Design Center with lots of natural light, open flexible space, comfortable seating, and several whiteboards for affixing/jotting notes, making it a perfect space for strategic thinking.

The book *Moments of Impact: How to Design Strategic Conversations That Accelerate Change*, by Chris Ertel and Lisa Kay Solomon (Simon & Schuster, 2014), is a good resource for conducting strategic planning sessions. In the book they state, "A great strategic conversation is not just an intellectual exercise—it's an exhilarating and memorable experience." You want the session to be an experience the participants will remember. For one thing, participants must feel the need for change. Consider incorporating role-playing or simulation exercises to work through alternatives. Sometimes a little thing can etch the experience in the minds of the participants. At the conclusion of one session, I handed out an electric candle to each participant with the final advice to go forth and shine light on their vision for others.

Think about who should be attending the session. While the board is ultimately responsible for the strategic plan, the session should involve other people with different perspectives. They suggest assembling a "dream team," including those with differing areas of expertise, differing roles within the organization, and representatives from all the demographics of your stakeholders. Hopefully, your board is diverse and represents a dream team already. They also recommend having a core group of those familiar with one another and supplemented by a few who are new. Including external participants as observers and listeners may be helpful. Multiple perspectives are key. In particular, staff should participate (not conduct) since they will be critical to execution. It is harder to be committed if you are not part of the conversation.

Kickoff

The leader of the session can be a member of the board or a hired facilitator, depending on who can most effectively run the session given the personalities in the room. The leader should open by explaining the objective of the session and where the group is expected to be at the end of the session. Data to prepare participants for the session may have been distributed for advance reading to save time and set a framework. A few ground rules should be established in the beginning to encourage strategic thinking and discussion.

- You will be conjuring up the future so there are no crazy thoughts or comments.
- To allow everyone to share their thoughts, the leader should recognize the person who will speak.

- Everyone is encouraged to question the status quo or current position and explore alternatives.

- Empathize with current and future stakeholders such as potential members, donors, beneficiaries, and service users. Put yourself in their place.

- Avoid groupthink or deferring to leaders.

- Listen, listen, listen—think of yourself as an observer in the balcony watching without bias from the outside, considering all viewpoints and perspectives.

Process

A well-planned, thorough, strategic planning process should be flexible and can be modified as you go for your group, but the order of review can be important. The following steps are meant to prevent putting "the cart before the horse." Often, the participants want to go straight to tactical steps before having a clear vision or to make decisions without understanding the environment or having sufficient data points. Figure 7.1 provides a step by step approach to strategic planning.

You may see different terminology, and not every group will define the steps the same way, so we will discuss what is meant by each.

Figure 7.1

SWOT Analysis

SWOT stands for strengths, weaknesses, opportunities, and threats. All stakeholders, including employees, should provide input as to what they see as strengths and weaknesses of the organization. This step answers the questions:

- Where are we now?
- What are the external trends that will impact our organization?
- What is changing?
- What is going on inside our organization, in our culture, and with our members that is impacting our organization?
- Which of our delivery and/or communication channels are most effective for each demographic?
- What are our participation trends?

Staff can provide data and conduct surveys or focus groups ahead of time. Engaging an independent survey firm may ensure unbiased outside perspective. More and more organizations are conducting surveys through-out the year, such as after events. Have staff summarize those surveys and identify any trends. Identify donors, staff, participants, members, and volunteers and interview them, either in a group setting or individually. It is important to get a representative group in each category, so you come to understand diverse perspectives. For example, be sure and interview those who were active and/or donors in the past but are not currently engaged financially or otherwise. Some sample questions to ask:

- Why did you participate, give, volunteer (tailor to the interviewee)?
- What activities did you participate in, and how did you hear about them?
- What can we do better?
- What is the best program or event we offer?
- What is your least favorite program or event and why?
- What additional programs would you like us to offer?
- What do you want the board to know as it embarks on strategic planning?

For opportunities and threats, it is important to look at whom you are competing with for the attention of your members, donors, or participants. If your organization has a competitor for members, grant funds, or donors, study the competition. What are they doing right? What are they doing differently, and how is it working for them? Try to gather their financial information from their website or their 990. Do they appear to be prospering and growing? How are they doing it? Are they reaching a demographic we want to reach but are not? Why is that?

As you look at the current environment facing your organization, you may want to invite outside experts to present the latest thinking on the needs you have met in the past. For example, a nonprofit credit union whose largest lending was for auto loans asked an expert on the future of self-driving cars and shared rides to come speak to its board. If you serve a certain demographic, you may request research on the impact of an economic downturn on the population you serve. If you are in the health-care field, you may want the latest health research on the segment you serve. For example, if you are focused on serving those facing breast cancer, you may want the latest research on diagnosis, cures, and treatment?

Once you are confident you have assessed the current strengths, weaknesses, opportunities, and threats, it is time to start thinking about the future.

Thinking Strategically

Asking the right questions at this point and asking the board and strategic planning committee to help develop a series of questions about the future at this point may get everyone thinking strategically. Example of questions to get them thinking might be the following:

- For continued success in fund-raising or program growth, what programs, services, or beneficiaries should be refined, expanded, or introduced?
- We can't do everything, so where should we focus our energies?
- What measures of success are most important to gauge our progress in moving toward our vision?
- How do we remain relevant to those we serve?

Mission

Now is the time to take a fresh look at your mission. Why does your organization exist? Why would someone want to get involved? What do we want to achieve and for whose benefit? Your mission statement should be concise and easily understood by your stakeholders. An example follows:

> The American Red Cross prevents and alleviates human suffering in the face of emergencies by mobilizing the power of volunteers and the generosity of donors.

The organization's mission is powerful and broad enough to cover its diverse program offerings. It even emphasizes the important roles of volunteers and donors. Start by listing key words and then wordsmith into a concise statement. The word "concise" has been used twice in this section for a reason. Every volunteer, particularly board members, needs to be able to share the mission in their "elevator speech" so that it rolls off their tongue each time they are asked about the organization.

Vision

Your vision reflects where your organization needs to go and what it will look like if effective and successful. Generally, you want to take a five-year view, but, with the accelerating speed of change, three years may be more realistic. Your vision should be aspirational but achievable. The best analogy may be building a house. You have a vision of what you want your house to look like from the street. Then you work with a builder and architect to draw up the plans. Your mission and vision should inspire support. In its vision statement, the American Red Cross states:

> We aspire to turn compassion into action so that
>
> > all people affected by disaster across the country and around the world receive care, shelter and hope;

our communities are ready and prepared for disasters;

everyone in our country has access to safe, lifesaving blood and blood products;

all members of our armed services and their families find support and comfort whenever needed; and

in an emergency, there are always trained individuals nearby, ready to use their Red Cross skills to save lives.

Your vision should think big. What could the organization achieve in the future? Don't get bogged down in resource constraints. Coming up with the needed resources is a tactical consideration. In the vision brainstorming session, ask everyone to dream and share their wishes for the organization. Assure everyone when they start that no suggestion is out of bounds. Then determine common themes and develop a shared vision supported by the entire board.

Values

Your values guide the work of the entire organization. They are not just the desires of the board and staff. They are the fundamental principles that your organization will live by. They are the shared beliefs of the stakeholders of the organization. The American Red Cross uses words like "humanity," "impartiality," "neutrality," "independence," "voluntary service," "unity," and "universality." It goes on to explain how each of those words applies to its organization.

To provide a slightly different perspective, the William & Mary Alumni Association (WMAA) values statement is as follows:

The William & Mary Alumni Association is the *independent* voice of alumni and friends and a *key influencer* for alumni engagement. We serve our *diverse* alumni population by providing a *welcoming* home for them when on campus; a network for career success; opportunities for personal connections and *relationships* no matter where they live. We foster a culture instilled while they are students, that alumni have a *responsibility* to care for and *nurture fellow alumni* and their alma mater. We will leverage technology for communications to encourage *engagement* and to create relevant programming. We will partner with chapters, affinity groups, university administration, and other constituent groups for *coordinated programming*. We will have alumni serving as advocates and *ambassadors* to enhance the brand and communicate the benefits of *lifelong* engagement with William & Mary. (emphasis added)

The WMAA board first listed the key words in italic font by the author and then created the paragraph to provide context. Again, once the key words are listed, note how often the individuals listed the same word or similar words. Those are the shared values of the leaders of the organization and, therefore, the organization itself.

Goals

Goals indicate how we get to our vision. What must be done to achieve our vision? The goals of the organization may have a short time frame such as two or three years. What are the priorities for the next few years going to be? First, you need to understand and discuss the options. Discuss *what we should do* and then *what we could do*. The group should examine all ideas and possibilities. What needs to happen for each option to be successful? Develop the alternatives and how they might play out.

Even more important, what do you need to stop doing? Often, boards just keep adding on without deleting, putting stress and strain on resources. Included in this step is an identification of resource needs, including people, technology, and money.

Once the most promising alternatives are identified, it is time to prioritize. To ensure that everyone has a voice, consider straw man votes. One organization gave everyone five dots and asked them to put their dots next to their five priorities. This allowed the group to visualize everyone's thoughts.

Goals need to be limited in number in order to be achievable. The board may want to establish a timeline for achieving the goals. For example, it may believe that certain goals need to be accomplished before others, or it may want to show progress, and some goals can be achieved quickly with larger impact, known as "the low-hanging fruit."

Tactics

Tactics are specific tasks that allow you to achieve your goals. Who will take what steps to accomplish the goal? When will it be done by, and what resources are required? In order to assign accountability and reporting responsibility, both a board member and a staff person should be listed. For example,

Goal: Use technology to attract younger volunteers

Tactic: Identify system applications to allow volunteers to sign up on their mobile devices

Responsibility: Board—vice president; staff—systems administrator

Completed by: March of current year

Resource needs: Intern to research available off-the-shelf applications

The next tactic under the goal may be to select and implement the application with a subsequent timeline and allocation of funds required for the purchase. Boards can get too much in the weeds here. In the aforementioned example, the board may want to discuss all the possible applications or the attributes of the system. This is better left for staff and any committee formed to accomplish the task.

Speaking of timelines, it is important to set deadlines, particularly short deadlines. As Robert Gates stated in *A Passion for Leadership*, "Short deadlines focus attention on an effort and signal its importance, creating momentum. . . . They also limit the time available for the opposition to coalesce and develop blocking strategies. . . . If I were limited to just one suggestion for implementing change in a bureaucracy, it would be to impose short deadlines on virtually every endeavor, deadlines that are enforced." Keeping the team focused on implementing the strategic plan can be challenging. Knowing they have a short deadline and that they will be reporting on progress (hopefully completion) at the deadline, keeps them accountable.

Metrics

The development of metrics is often overlooked in the strategic planning process. Certainly, deadlines are a metric. However, the best practice for metrics is to step back and determine what the impact on the organization will be by accomplishing the goals. Continuing the aforementioned example, how many new young volunteers have signed up using the mobile application? Did they volunteer for more than one event and over multiple years? Did they make a financial donation? Key performance indicators such as these should be identified and then reported on at each board meeting. Posting a dashboard of the metrics on the organization's website is a great way of keeping the key performance indicators in front of the board, its volunteers, and all the stakeholders. It also builds excitement as goals are accomplished. Sending periodic blasts directing the stakeholders to the website to see the progress and encourage participation is also important. Use graphics and fun charts to convey your excitement of what has been accomplished.

Evaluation and Next Steps

First of all, do not push for next steps until you have consensus on your strategic plan. Pause here and ask the group if they are excited about what they have accomplished during their planning session(s). Remember that you may need to break the aforementioned steps into multiple sessions to give everyone time to gather additional data or think about what has been decided. Those sessions should be held within a month or so of each other in order not to lose momentum.

In *Moments of Impact: How to Design Strategic Conversations That Acceler-ate Change*, the authors discuss eight Key "Planks" to a Common Plat-form. In evaluating your strategic planning, ask yourselves if you have the following:

1. Sense of shared purpose
2. Sense of group identity and community
3. Common understanding of challenges
4. Sense of urgency
5. Shared language system/common definition of key terms
6. Shared base of information to draw on
7. Capacity to discuss tough issues
8. Common frames through which to see the issues

If your board can answer "yes" to these, it has not only a good strategic plan but also a great working relationship to move forward as a board.

Communication

Once the board finalizes the strategy, its next decision is how to commu-nicate the strategy to get buy-in and build excitement. Even though you con-sulted with many stakeholders, they need to be informed about the final strategic plan. One option is to discuss each goal, with changes planned one at a time to not overwhelm everyone.

The alternative is to announce the plan with great fanfare, building momentum for the future. Often goals are intertwined and need to all be implemented to achieve the vision. This would support making a big dra-matic announcement laying out all the plans and explaining how they work together to move the organization forward. As Robert Gates stated in *A Pas-sion for Leadership*, "Announcing initiatives all at once reduces uncertainty about hidden agendas or future surprises. Whatever apprehension employ-ees feel can be mitigated by making clear that they all will have the opportu-nity to help shape the actual implementation."

Informing the broad constituency of the plan will most likely involve cov-erage in the media, internal and external, including social media. Curate the conversation emphasizing the positive impact expected from the initiatives. Announce those audacious goals asking for everyone to play a role in achiev-ing them. If components are expected to be controversial, consult with a public relations firm to determine how best to address such issues. Explain-ing the "whys" of certain controversial decisions as well as the process for making the decision may sway the naysayers.

Updating the Plan

Your plan is a living document that should be reevaluated annually. Set aside a meeting, or retreat approximately one year from your original planning session. Prior to the session, ask each board or staff member responsible for a task or tactic to report to the board the progress toward completing the task and achieving the goal. Ask them to delineate any changes in facts, obstructions or road blocks encountered, reactions from stakeholders, and changes in resource needs and conclude with any recommendations that need to be brought to the board's attention.

At the annual strategic plan review, begin by establishing the objectives for the day. Remember you are not redoing the planning process. After one year, you are evaluating only progress and reminding everyone of what the organization set out to do a year ago. The objectives for the update are as follows:

- Revisit the organization's strategy and direction considering internal and external influences over the past year that are impacting the organization.
- Set priorities for the coming year.
- Update the tasks or tactics, eliminating ones that were accomplished and adding follow-up tasks to move the organization forward.
- Provide continuity since a portion of the board rotates off each year and a new group of board members is added.
- Continue to drive and implement the strategy.
- Review the work accomplished over the past year against the plan.
- Determine what worked and what didn't work.
- Add new ideas and new points of view, particularly from new board members.

It is helpful for the strategic planning chair to reach out to new board members to get them up to speed prior to the planning session, or they may hold a conference call for all new board members and review the vision, goals, and objectives and tasks/tactics from the prior year. Once the entire board or planning task force is convened, refresh everyone's memory on the overall objectives. One organization then broke into smaller groups, one for each objective, with a facilitator/scribe for each objective. Each group had a set amount of time to discuss the objective and suggest new priorities or tasks to move further toward achieving the goals and objectives. The suggested priorities or tasks were put on a flip chart. Each group then rotated so that each group got to discuss what was put on the flip chart by the previous group and agree or disagree. By breaking into smaller groups, there was more opportunity for discussion and for new board members to ask questions. They were asked to rank the priorities in order of importance to the organization.

At the end of the day, the tasks with the highest number of votes were discussed and agreed on by the entire group. The strategic planning chair then met with the executive committee to determine responsibilities and general timelines. New task force committees were needed for some tasks allowing for new board members to become engaged. Also new chairs for the task force committees were needed in some situations.

What was important is that there was new buy-in and enthusiasm for the strategic plan. The board felt a sense of accomplishment when it focused on just how much has been achieved over the past year. The vision continued to be the guiding principle, and any variations to the prior year plan were well thought out. They were not just "oh that didn't work so let's try this." Everyone understood why a course correction was needed and agreed on the path forward.

Reality Check

The trade association had a new leadership who immediately recognized that their organization was stagnant. Membership was holding its own but aging. Younger people were not joining or, if their parents got them to join, were not participating. The association needed a reinvigorating spark. The board leadership knew that while the organization had made several attempts at strategic planning over the years, the plan had long sat on the shelf and was not a living document. It always identified the same problems but no action to address the problems. Also, the financial sustainability of some of the programs was in question due to changes in demographics and affordability of the programs. On the positive side, participation in and quality of the programs were trending up. A new vice president of development had taken the initiative to create new giving opportunities, so contributions to their foundation were increasing significantly.

The time was right to begin a new strategic planning process. First, a strategic planning task force made up of previous leaders of strategic planning efforts and the executive committee of the board met prior to a board meeting. Copies of prior plans and participation analyses were distributed. The task force agreed to update the previous survey data. It became clear from the initial meeting that a new approach to strategic planning was needed to effect change. It was decided that the board officers and the vice president of programming, along with the executive director, would lead the effort. They became the strategic planning leaders.

That group was encouraged to read *Moments of Impact: How to Design Strategic Conversations That Accelerate Change*. The leaders had several phone conferences to discuss how to approach the process. They spent a lot of time identifying who should participate in the session or sessions in order to get diverse perspectives, including historical perspectives as well as those of the younger members they needed to attract. Staff were to be included. Invitations were extended. An offsite location and date were reserved. Survey questions were drafted and redrafted. Much debate among the leaders ensued about how much information to provide in advance with the concern expressed that they might bias thinking. Ultimately, the survey results were provided in advance.

Predicting the future is difficult, so one leader was tasked with preparing a presentation on what thought leaders were saying about the future. Another presentation about the differences among generations was prepared. On the evening prior to the planning session, the participants met in a private room at a restaurant and, after drinks, were assigned seats to ensure diverse perspectives in each group. The plan was to get through the identification of goals by end of the session the following day. That evening, the presentations on the future as well as generational differences were made and allowed to "percolate" overnight. The groups were each given provocative questions about the value of the organization to discuss and then report out on in the form of a newspaper headline about the organization five years in the future.

The next morning, the entire group listened as each group reported out its headline. It was entertaining but did not accomplish the strategic leaders' goal of building a vision. It did accomplish the goal of making the process a memorable experience. The groups from the prior evening were then assigned a generational age group and an exercise that would allow them to empathize with or get into the mind-set of that age group. Using that mind-set, they developed a list of the strengths, weaknesses, opportunities, and threats for the association. Each group then presented its top five points in each category.

During lunch, the leaders took the resulting comments and developed common themes. The entire group then discussed the common themes to be developed into five overarching values or strategic imperatives. Consensus was built among the strategic imperatives and the fact that the existing mission was generally still good. There was time left only for participants to break up into groups for each strategic imperative and brainstorm about potential tactics. It was agreed to meet again in a couple months to address goals and tactics.

The leaders discussed all the results of the session and decided that the best approach was to provide for discussion at the next session a slightly revised mission, values/strategic imperatives, and priorities or goals for the next two years. Many conference calls resulted in a document distributed to the rest of the group prior to their next session.

At the second session, alternatives were discussed. Compromises occurred, and consensus was built. A road map, including resource needs, was developed. More refinement of the tactics was required, but everyone left feeling they had accomplished something no prior board had achieved. Change would happen.

CHAPTER EIGHT

The Big Event

An important part of every nonprofit's calendar are events, some small such as bake sales and some large such as the Winter Games for Special Olympics. Each requires leadership and organization to be successful. This chapter discusses the basics of event planning that can be scaled up or down depending on the size of the event. The board should always provide oversight and show commitment by participating. In addition, it is the board's responsibility to evaluate whether the event met its mission, is consistent with the mission of the organization, and is worth the effort required to conduct it. Often events just keep getting added on, overloading volunteers and staff. Someone gets the board excited about an opportunity and off we go. Instead, a disciplined approach is required as outlined beginning with the decision to hold the event.

Why Should the Event Be Held?

Before deciding to undertake the planning of an event, the board should determine and document the purpose of the planned event. Is it to further the programmatic offerings of the organization? For example, a new leadership training event in a new location for a nonprofit that offers training would expand the reach and program offerings of that organization. Is it to raise awareness of the organization? An example would be a booth at a community festival where brochures about how to get involved with the organization are distributed. Is it to raise funds for the nonprofit? From black-tie dinners to bake sales to runs and walks, these are all examples of events that raise funds. Sometimes the best events accomplish all three purposes. A weekend (see Reality Check later) that brings your organization to its constituents may offer programming, inspire sponsorship, and bring awareness to those who have not felt engaged.

Who will benefit from the event? Are they our stakeholders? A particular event may benefit a great cause such as funding schools in India, but if the organization's mission is supporting athletes in Maryland high schools, it probably should not be undertaken. Once the purpose is clearly defined, the board can decide if the event's purpose is consistent with the mission and image of the organization. A casino night might be fun, but is its image appropriate for a youth organization?

Also, does it compete with other programs or activities that would impact participation? Can it fill an open slot in the calendar, or will it replace an event that has declining participation or is not a current focus of the organization? Is it an event that will attract volunteers to get involved? Once these questions are answered at the board level, the board can vote on proceeding with the next step, event planning.

Planning

Ideally an event committee comprised of a board liaison, volunteers and staff should perform the planning. Just as a board should be selected to ensure a variety of expertise and skill sets, the committee should also comprise the required skill sets to plan and execute the event. Required skills include finance, event planning, marketing, public relations, social media, and fund-raising. These may need to be supplemented with logistics and facilities, community relations, catering, and any others depending on the nature of the event. The chair(s) should be selected/elected. Consideration should be given to the selection of honorary chairs, who are selected because of their status in the community or willingness to be a major sponsor. Typically, the honorary chair(s) are not involved in the execution of the event but serve as advisors and make connections for the organization.

If this is a recurring event, it is important to get fresh perspectives by adding new volunteers to the committee joining experienced volunteers. Before beginning the planning, the board liaison should provide an orientation, including the purpose of the event and any other critical success factors. If this is a repeat event, an evaluation of the prior year event, including strengths, weaknesses, opportunities, and threats, should be conducted and shared.

Next, ask the committee to develop a vision for the event. Just like in strategic planning, now is the time to dream about what you want the event to look like, consistent with its mission. This may lead to a discussion of a theme for the event.

Now that the why is covered, the committee can begin discussing the who, what, when, and where. The *"who"* includes all stakeholders. Who are the likely attendees, sponsors, volunteers, and beneficiaries?

What are the ideas for the event programs and activities? With the vision and mission in mind, brainstorm about the programs, ancillary activities, speakers, and so on. If the event is a multiday event, consider an opening or keynote event. It is imperative that the activities provide an experience the participants cannot get elsewhere. A higher ticket price can be charged for exclusive activities such as behind-the-scenes tours or high-profile speaker. You may want to consider the diversity of the audience and ensure activities that appeal to all demographics are included. List all suggestions and the required contact information. Who in the organization knows the person who can make this activity happen or speaker appear? If the list is long, consider having the committee rank in priority the activities they are most interested in. It may be appropriate to pause and have staff or volunteers investigate the feasibility of the highest-ranked activities. Consider events to thank your sponsors and volunteers. Sponsors will often receive certain benefits for their sponsorship, including a special thank-you event.

When should the event be held? Allow enough time for planning, scheduling, hiring of caterers/performers, renting of the venue, and so on. Major events take a year to plan.

Depending on how complex the event is, numerous subcommittees may be required. For example, a festival may have subcommittees for educational exhibits, development/fund-raising, security, food, art, concert, and so on.

Where the event should be held is normally dependent on the nature of the event. Consider the number of attendees and capacity of the facility. Is the space flexible with walls that can be opened or closed if the needs change? If the venue is too large, it will appear that more were expected than showed up. Remember to include capacity for special guests such as sponsors, speakers, and community officials. Is there pre-function space for a pre-event reception? Is there a catering kitchen or meal preparation area if an outside caterer is contemplated? Cost and availability also need to be considered. Is there a facility willing to donate the space if a certain food and beverage minimum is met? If there is a strong preference for a particular caterer, where do they have relationships? Some facilities have a required vendor list. Will audiovisual services be required? If so, some facilities require that you use their internal service, often at an inflated cost. If alcohol will be served, who will meet the state licensing and insurance requirements? Negotiating the use of facilities and reviewing the agreement may require legal advice. At a minimum, legal counsel and the organization's insurance broker should review all agreements prior to signing. Another issue to be addressed relates to ensuring there is handicapped accessibility at all venues.

Risk Management and Insurance

As plans are being developed for the event, it is important that the risks surrounding the event be evaluated. It is not a good idea to hold a fundraiser that is a skeet shooting event and serve alcohol (yes, that was a real situation). Activities such as carnival or other rides provided by a third-party might sound like good family fun. However, the licensing and inspection requirements as well as a somewhat poor reputation of some providers should give you pause before pursuing such activities. One Virginia festival planned to offer helicopter rides. However, after considering the risks and the bad publicity a recent accident had generated, the decision was made to cancel that activity.

Auctions are a popular component of many fund-raiser events. The items included in the auction also need to be evaluated to determine their risk. Even though an outsider donates the activity or item, if anyone is injured or worse, the organization may be held liable and, in any case, may receive negative publicity. Organizations may want to decline accepting the donation of medical treatments, for example. Cosmetic procedures, which used to be a popular donation item, should be avoided in today's litigious society.

Review the organization's insurance to be sure the event is covered under the liability policy. If the event is being held at a private residence, ensure there is adequate coverage to protect the homeowner. All it takes is one situation to destroy a relationship. One recent experience involved a home tour where a board member and major donor offered her home. An attendee slipped on the property and was injured. This led to a lawsuit with both the homeowner's insurance and the organization's insurance claiming the other party was responsible. Unfortunately, the organization lost a major donor and board member in the process. This could have been avoided with a clearly written agreement and investigation of coverage in advance of the event. If alcohol will be served, be sure and investigate the liquor liability insurance coverage. Each caterer and the organization should have adequate coverage and add the other as additional insured.

Organization

The committee structure can be expanded or reduced depending on the complexity of the event. It is important from the beginning to understand the role of staff versus the volunteer. If there are staff who have responsibility for event planning and management, then the board and event committee can focus on oversight, conceptual planning, and fund-raising. Alternatively, if staff is limited, a volunteer structure must be developed to ensure a successful event. The board should get regular updates as the planning progresses. The event committee and its subcommittees should prepare monthly summaries of plans and their status for the board. The role of affiliated organizations should also be defined. How much input will they have into the programming for the event, and will they provide financial support?

Budget and Finance

Before the planning committee makes any commitments, a budget must be drafted. If there are subcommittees, it may be appropriate for each to submit a budget request for their area. If this is a recurring event, the actual revenues and expenditures for prior events may be used as a guide. A budget and finance subcommittee could be formed to have responsibility for budget development and financial reporting.

Consider all sources of revenue, including ticket sales, sponsorships, community grants, rental fees, advertising revenue, and other revenues. Some revenue may be in-kind revenue, such as donated facilities, auction items, or advertising. These can be included in revenue but must then also be included in expenditures. Estimate the number of tickets to be sold for each event (free tickets for sponsors and honored guests should not be included). Estimate the sponsorship income and contributions. Is there a government or related organization that will award a grant for the event? Can the organization charge rental fees for booths or exhibition space at the event? Will there be a program or newsletter that advertising space can be sold for? Other revenue might be from auctions, live or silent, or a "raise the paddle." Live and silent auctions can make an event exciting and generate significant revenue but tend to be labor intensive. These were discussed further in Chapter 4 on fund-raising.

Expenditures include the following:

- Facilities rental, including parking
- Food and beverage costs
- Labor for outside services, such as security and parking
- Travel and lodging
- Audiovisual costs
- Printing
- Decorations, table linens, tables/chairs, and floral
- Auction items that are purchased
- Supplies
- Advertising and website fees
- Transportation such as buses to transport attendees from remote parking to activities
- Auction or other outsourced technology administrators
- Credit card fees
- Speaker honorariums or thank-you gifts for speakers and sponsors, if any
- Awards or other program-related costs

- Golf cart rental to expedite movement of key volunteers if venue is large
- Postage, shipping, packaging costs
- Other expenditures

Each of the aforementioned expenditures, which are not an exhaustive list, needs to be budgeted based on contract bids, research, or prior year. It may be helpful to classify by specific activity, so you can be sure the activity revenues support the expenditures or have sponsorship support. Keeping in mind the purpose of the event, the budget should generally reflect revenues equal to expenditures, or if the purpose is to raise funds, then the overall fund-raising goal should equal the excess of revenues over expenditures. Once the budget is developed, the board or its designee should approve it. As new contracts are approved and new information is gained, it may be necessary to modify the budget. Each person responsible for a budgeted area should be informed of the budget expectations and held responsible for any variances. The budget is a working document. As expenditures are incurred and revenues are collected, the actual revenues and expenditures should be reported in comparison with the budget and variances explained. Transparency with the board is critical, so there are no surprises.

Fund-Raising and Sponsorship

The first stop for fund-raising and sponsorship should be the organization's board. Each board member should be expected to be a sponsor at the level they are capable of as well as recruit their friends to be sponsors. They are also responsible along with the planning or event committee with getting attendees to the event through personal invitations. Many have a policy of asking event committee members to financially support the event as well.

Sponsorship solicitation is often the responsibility of a development sub-committee along with development staff. Solicitation approaches differ depending on whether you are asking a corporation or an individual. For each, the benefits need to be considered and included in the brochure and electronic publications.

Sponsorship Levels

With an event, sponsors can be attracted to new or higher levels of giving based on benefits they receive. The decision as to the levels of recognition and the benefits received should be made carefully to ensure each level is distinctive and the benefits are not excessive. One recent event found out too late that the number of tickets being given away to sponsors as a benefit exceeded the capacity of the event. Be creative in naming the levels consistent with the theme of the event. Typical benefits include special sponsor–only events. These tend to be the greatest incentive for the higher levels of giving, so it needs to be exclusive to those in the top three tiers. A book signing, "meet and greet" with the keynote speaker, and a patron's dinner at a private residence are examples of exclusive events. Special-themed gifts can also be considered but are less in favor, as individuals seem to want less "stuff." Recognition in community newspapers, websites, and programs with all levels listed is important, as well as recognition on signage at the event. If there are multiple activities, the opportunity to sponsor an individual activity is available, with the price of sponsorship set based on the attendance and visibility of the event. The IRS requires disclosure of the value of the benefits received with each contribution or sponsorship so that the donor understands that the amount available to take as a tax-deductible contribution is net of the value of those benefits. It is best to consult with a tax expert when developing the disclosure.

Corporate Sponsorship

Major corporations often have foundations focused on particular charitable priorities such as education or community. In order to successfully approach them, you need an advocate within the corporation to promote the funding by the foundation. Again, look to the board and the event committee to identify relationships with key decision makers at the corporation. Prepare a written proposal that portrays how the event benefits the cause that the corporate foundation prioritizes for support.

Alternatively, a corporation may be interested in gaining publicity and marketing benefits for its products or services. Gaining this type of sponsorship still is more likely with a relationship inside the corporation. In this situation, you are asking for a portion of the marketing or advertising budget, so the sooner you ask, the better, ideally prior to the corporation's budget development. Understand the benefits a corporation may want, such as tickets to the event to entertain clients, a booth to distribute samples or brochures, and inclusion in the program. Again, a well-thought-out written proposal will increase the chances of success in gaining a significant sponsorship. Consider the appropriateness of the corporate sponsor for the event. For example, it may not be a good idea for a beer distributor to sponsor a youth-focused event.

Individual Sponsorship

Asking for individual sponsorships is similar to asking for major gifts but with benefits provided to the individual. Develop a list of likely sponsors and who should make the ask. While the focus may be on major gifts and high-level sponsors, participation is also important, and not all members of the events committee may have the capacity to make a major gift. Have a category of "friends" who make a contribution and deserve to be recognized but whose contribution is not of the level specified for benefits.

Auctions/Raffles

As mentioned earlier, auctions have become increasingly popular activities for event-related fund-raising. The items must be unique and not someone's discards. Remember, auctions are part of the entertainment, so the number of items auctioned, particularly in a live auction, should be limited to less than 20 for a live auction and two or three times that for a silent auction. There are now firms that will administer the auction from electronic bidding via a smartphone to automatic charging of payment to the successful bidder's credit card, all for a flat fee and/or percentage of the proceeds. An easier way to generate extra funds is a "raise the paddle," Attendees are given a paddle with their assigned number. The auctioneer discusses a particular cause and then starts the bidding at a high amount such as $5,000, and anyone willing to donate that amount raises their paddle. The auctioneer then moves to a lower amount, and others willing to donate at that level raise their paddles and so on down to $100 or whatever amount the demographics of the audience supports. Speaking of auctioneer, having one who is a local celebrity and understands the importance of adding humor and playing up competition among bidders will increase funds generated and the overall experience. This is not a time to worry about serving alcohol since revenues raised tend to go up with consumption. Raffles are another option for adding revenue to an event. They are often governed by state law, so be sure to understand the governing regulations. For each of these activities, having the participation of beneficiaries of the organization such as students and athletes adds to the excitement and amounts generated. Decide whether you will allow remote bidding, which smartphone technology now supports. If remote bids are permitted, clarify how the successful bidder will pick up the items and make sure they understand their credit card will be charged the night of the event.

Raffles are another popular event-related fund-raising activity. The first step when considering holding a raffle is to investigate state laws surrounding raffles. Some states prohibit or sharply limit them. The items being raffled off need to be evaluated for risk, just as auction items do. The details and requirements for the "prize" need to be clearly spelled out. For example, don't promote that you are raffling off a car if you are really raffling a three-year lease. If the winner is responsible for certain fees, that should be clearly disclosed. The great thing about raffles is that they can be promoted in advance of the event so that even those who cannot attend the event can participate.

Communications, Marketing, and Social Media

How are you going to promote your event? As soon as the date is finalized, sending a "save the date" and announcing the event in all of the organization's publications is the first step. The subcommittee should develop a communication plan that includes timeline and potential mediums, electronic and print. If this is a community-wide event, local media outlets may be willing to donate advertising/promotional time and space via in-kind media time contribution. They each have websites, so make sure coverage includes their websites. A public relations plan should be developed getting the event chair, keynote speaker, board chair, and so on interviewed in the local media. If the event spans several days, applications can be downloaded to smartphones that provide reminders of the activities, allow donations and registration, and provide the latest updates on logistical and program topics. Are there blogs that might promote the event because it supports the cause they blog about? How is real-time coverage of the event by the press being handled? The subcommittee should think about what real or perceived threats to participation might be and ensure publicity addresses those threats. For example, if parking might be a challenge, communicate all the options, including mass transportation. Ensure there are younger members on the communications subcommittee to provide input on how to reach their peers through social media. However, never forget that not everyone uses technology, so communication through newsletters, mail, and printed invitations should also be included.

The Big Event

After all the planning, communication, and organization, it is finally time for the event. Ensure key vendors, volunteers, and staff have one another's contact information. Provide the complete detailed schedule, with staff or volunteers responsible for each event as well as any logistical information. If a multiday event, schedule nightly debriefing sessions, reviewing how the day went and plans for the following day. Ensure honorary guests and speakers have escorts responsible for getting them to the appropriate venues well in advance of the start. Say thank-you often to volunteers, staff, and attendees. Continue building excitement, and keep the energy level high. The board should be visible and constant cheerleaders.

Event Evaluation

Shortly after the event and after everyone has caught up on their sleep but memories and thoughts are fresh, begin the evaluation process. Immediately send surveys to volunteers and participants that are short and can be completed in about five minutes, but provide an opportunity to add comments. There are multiple vehicles such as Survey Monkey that provide a survey service electronically for free. One of the best approaches is to develop a net promoter score with the results. The questions are structured so that the responder indicates, on a scale of 1 to 10, how likely they are to attend the event again and if they would recommend the event to a friend. Adding a few other questions, such as where they heard about the event and what value they received from participating, will also provide helpful data for future events.

The survey software compiles the results, which can then be shared with the board and event committee. The event committee should then meet and discuss the survey results, what went well, and what should be done differently in the future. Document recommendations for improvement. Are there activities that should be dropped or vendors that should not be used again? Document, document, document. Most important, did the event fulfill its mission? Did it enhance the image of the organization? Was it worth the effort? Would the volunteers sign up again? It may take a few weeks to get the final financial results, so this meeting may focus on the nonfinancial impact of the event. Subject to the final accounting of the financial success, would the committee recommend to the board that the event be repeated? Hopefully the enthusiasm is high, and the committee will recommend that the event become part of the "traditions" of the organization.

After the Event Recognition

Everyone is basking in the glow of the success of the event, and they are exhausted. But there is still more work to be done. Volunteers need to be thanked, and you may want to have a small event to thank them and get them excited to volunteer again next year. You may want to send a small token recognizing those who have volunteered repeatedly or chaired a committee.

Acknowledgments for sponsors and donors need to be drafted and sent. For donors, the amount of the ticket price or portion (if any) of auction item proceeds that represent the value received should be delineated. Always include a statement that the donor should consult with their own tax advisor. The organization should not be seen as giving tax advice.

Reality Check

How exciting! The international council of a prestigious health organization had selected Williamsburg for its annual meeting. It would provide the U.S. chapter the opportunity to host international dignitaries and showcase its activities as well as the beautiful historic area. Because the meeting was held each year in a different country, there was always a desire to provide grander experiences for the council members and their spouses and guests. The bad news was that the host chapter was required to fund the costs of the five-day event that culminated in a black-tie dinner. The U.S. chapter needed a budget as soon as possible in order to figure out how to fund the meeting. In addition, due to staff turnover, there were only four staff members, and they had all been with the organization less than a year. The chair for the region considered the dignitaries (including royalty) likely to attend along with the limited staff resources and recommended the hiring of a consultant to administratively chair the event. The U.S. chapter board hired an experienced consultant.

An event volunteer leadership team consisting of the regional chair and a well-connected local member was assembled. The event committee under its leadership included a former U.S. chapter chair, a new high-energy member of the organization with event planning expertise, a member responsible for transportation of key dignitaries, a member responsible for activities related to the veteran's hospital, a member responsible for the black-tie dinner, and a member responsible for a special tour of Jamestown due to his connections there. It was expected that other Virginia members would volunteer and be used the week of the event. However, without specific duties assigned well in advance, they made other plans. Step one now was providing attractive materials about the meeting a year in advance to the council at their annual meeting in South Africa. Since attendance was limited, a communications/marketing committee was not necessary. Materials were gathered from Colonial Williamsburg, which would be the venue for most of the events, and the executive director of the U.S. chapter ensured that the expected schedule and the attractive Colonial Williamsburg and Jamestown pictures were presented in a flyer distributed in South Africa.

A meeting was held with the president of Colonial Williamsburg, the president of its hotel division, and the director of its events department. Impressing on them the importance of hosting this high-profile organization and group of dignitaries and providing them the opportunity to use photos in their publications after the event as well as offering a special event for their board or donors resulted in gaining their cooperation and the commitment of the president. It also helped that a major donor and member of their board was a member of the organization. (*USE* those relationships!) The chapter board chair, staff, the consultant, and the event leadership chair met and conducted a site visit. A vision for the meeting (the purpose was defined by the organization's legal documents) was developed by this group. Ideas for events for the attendees were listed, and the dates were finalized. Relationships and connections were called on to develop unique experiences worthy of the dignitaries while showcasing the best of the historic area. The chapter board chair was convinced that funds could be raised to cover the cost of the meeting by inviting sponsors to attend the nonbusiness events and dinners with the dignitaries. He agreed to contact key members and invite their sponsorship. The budget was further refined and presented to the U.S. chapter board for approval. Contracts for lodging, private tours, transportation, and food and beverage were negotiated and executed. Insurance issues were addressed. Various protocols were determined and distributed. Foreign embassies were contacted. Security issues at all venues had to be addressed. The consultant kept documenting the details of the schedule along with contact information and responsibilities, including assigning escorts/drivers. Dinner speakers were contacted, and ideas were provided for their remarks. This was truly an event where "the devil was in the details." Due to the small size of the event committee and staff, calls were held weekly to ensure progress. The executive director set timelines for completion of materials for printing, which then set deadlines for other items such as menus and activity programs. Yes, there were hiccups, last-minute changes, volunteers disagreeing with each other, surprise costs, and so on, but we kept our vision in focus and worked through it all. The executive director ruled with firm hand and ensured we stayed within budget. Others helped with publicizing the opportunity to be a sponsor and attend a once-in-a-lifetime event. The sponsorship goal was surpassed (which was good because last-minute audiovisual costs exceeded budget). Last-minute handicapped accessibility issues were dealt with.

The week of the event, the attendees arrived from all over the world and were warmly greeted sailing through a smooth registration process. Respecting the long travel distance and various time zones they came from, the plan was to start with low-key activities that oriented them to the historic area and then build throughout the week and culminate with the black-tie dinner in the garden of the Governor's Palace.

What particularly helped in delivering a quality event was having a partnership with Colonial Williamsburg and our other venues' leadership with a common vision for a very high-quality event. Several times when the leadership team suggested cutting something to save costs, venue management offered to absorb the cost to ensure an "over-the-top" experience. Each day the consultant distributed a pocket guide for the day with a detailed schedule and contact information for each activity. This came in handy when a fire alarm went off at a museum where a spouse/sponsor tour was planned.

U.S. sponsors stepped in to help host the hospitality suite, push wheelchairs, and help our small event committee wherever necessary. Each evening the event committee met to identify issues, discuss the next day, and share any feedback. Most important, because we took a personal approach to the event, each attendee felt we went above and beyond in hosting them for the event. True Southern hospitality was shared, and everyone was treated as royalty, whether they were or not. The feedback from attendees was extremely positive, and many friendships were formed.

While it should be several years before the United States hosts the meeting again, everything was documented as a guide for the future.

CHAPTER NINE

How Are We Doing as a Board?

High-performing boards never accept the status quo. They pursue continuous improvement. In order for the organization to continuously improve, the board itself must continuously improve. The starting point for that is regular self-assessments. These self-assessments should be done of the board meetings, its committees, the board as a whole, and each board member individually.

Multiple tools are available for conducting board assessments. In recent years, technology has facilitated assessments allowing board members to complete assessments online, with the software summarizing the results for analysis. The range of options is free services such as Survey Monkey to industry-specific mobile applications that can be completed on their smartphone on the plane ride home.

Considering analysis, there is no reason to conduct the assessment if the results are not analyzed and acted on for improvement. Who is responsible for that analysis along with the development of action steps for improvement? Generally, the board development or governance committee has the responsibility in conjunction with the board chair or president. Staff may suggest and arrange for board training in areas where the board is lacking skills and knowledge.

While board meetings should be evaluated at the conclusion of each board meeting, the other formal evaluations are generally performed on an annual basis. That does not prevent informal evaluations and performance discussions on an as-needed basis, particularly as it relates to individual board members.

Assessing How We Are Going to Work Together

With new board members typically joining the board each year, the dynamics of how the board works together change. Leadership styles vary with personalities. While team-building exercises may help build relationships among board members, understanding the personality traits and leadership styles may provide insight into how the board members are most comfortable communicating with each other, which board members need detailed analytical data, and which prefer to make decisions based on more emotional, subjective information. Understanding personality and leadership traits may also be useful in making committee assignments. Certain traits may be more valuable on a finance committee than, say, a committee like communications that may require a more creative thinker. There are no wrong styles. Over the past 50 years a variety of tests have been developed and refined to assess personality and leadership traits.

Technology is also available to assess the personality, leadership traits, learning approaches, and so on of your board members in order for them to understand how to work best with each other. Investing in these assessments when there are new board members each year may facilitate a smooth transition. Understanding how each board member approaches decision-making, for example, may make them more tolerant of the process a board member is comfortable with prior to making a decision. Examples of such personal assessments are Myers Briggs Personality Test and DiSC©. While the following provides a general sense of the tests, it is critical that trained test administrators be engaged by the organization to analyze and facilitate what the results mean for your organization.

The Myers Briggs tests divide personalities into four general areas, indicating natural tendencies on spectrums within those areas. The first area is where do you get your energy, internally or externally. Are you extraverted or introverted? The second area is how you understand things. Are you more sensing or intuitive? The third area relates to how you make decisions. Are you more focused on the facts and logic or more sensitive and rely on personal feelings? The fourth area relates to how you are comfortable taking action. Do you want to plan things out, or are you more comfortable proceeding without a plan?

The DISC© personality test classifies the individual on a spectrum for four factors: dominance, influence, steadiness, and compliance. Within those factors are behavior styles on a spectrum. Under dominance, a person can be analytical and assertive, very assertive or assertive and persuasive. Under influence, the spectrum is assertive and persuasive, very persuasive or supportive and persuasive. Under steadiness, a person can be supportive and persuasive, very supportive or supportive and analytical, which leaves compliance with a spectrum of supportive and analytical, very analytical or analytical and assertive. Ideally a board or committee will benefit from members across the spectrums. They can each play different roles based on their behavior styles.

These are two examples of assessments that provide indications of how a board member might communicate or prefer to be communicated with. They also indicate how analytical, extroverted, introverted, social, and reflective they are. For example, do they adapt well to change, or do they prefer one-on-one communication to group communication. Understanding each other facilitates a highly functioning board.

Many see these assessments as a benefit of board service since they increase their personal understanding. They can use the results in all facets of their life.

Tests can be taken online but are most effective when the results are discussed one on one with a testing consulting expert. The consultant can meet with each board member and then also meet with the group as a whole to portray where board members fit on the spectrum. The consultant can also recommend ways for the diverse types to work together.

Individual Board Member Assessment

It is rare for every member of the board to meet all the requirements for strong board participation. However, lack of engagement by a board member jeopardizes the effectiveness of the board in achieving its goals. For example, if several board members do not attend board meetings, a quorum may not be present to conduct the business of the organization. If board members do not contribute financially, they are not setting the proper standard to ask others to contribute.

Problems with individual board members can often be prevented, with clear expectations documented and discussed with prospective board members prior to asking them to serve. Written expectations should include the number of board and committee meetings they are expected to attend and whether they can participate by phone. Giving-level expectations should include attendance and sponsorship at fund-raising events. Again the board must set an example for other volunteers. The roles of board members in evaluating the executive director or president of the organization and determining their compensation should be listed along with clearly explaining the staff versus board relationship. Financial and strategic oversight responsibilities should be included in the document as well. Requirements to sign a conflict of interest policy with an explanation of what is a conflict of interest and how any potential conflicts should be disclosed and resolved should also be included. Standards for professional conduct, including all types of harassment, should be covered just as it is for employees of the organization.

Addressing issues with a board member is sensitive, especially since they are probably donors or community leaders and have deep relationships within the organization. The responsibility for addressing issues rests with the president or chair of the board. It is better to address the issue early rather than wait until the end of the year or when they are being considered for an additional term. For example, if a new board member misses a meeting and does not provide an appropriate explanation and follow any policies for advising the board chair in advance, the chair should contact that board member. An additional effective strategy for ensuring high performance from board members is to assign a mentor to all new board members for their first year. As discussed in Chapter 2, the mentor can reach out to the new board member in advance of all meetings to inquire if they received the advance materials and reviewed them. They can then follow up after the board meeting to see how the new board member is feeling about their service. Often reiterating expectations and reinforcing them during training can prevent issues.

All board members should be made to feel comfortable in the meetings and in social events and activities where they are expected to participate. If one board member dominates the discussion, makes inappropriate remarks, or does not conduct themselves appropriately, immediate action must be taken. The severity of the conduct determines the level of action to be taken. For example, if a board member has too much to drink and makes inappropriate remarks to another board member, this is considered a form of harassment. Warnings and special training may be called for. If the behavior is severe and/or repetitive, the board member should be asked to resign. It is best to consult with legal counsel in these matters. A board member is responsible for the conduct of their spouse or guest. If an issue arises with them, it must be addressed by the board member.

Sometimes board members join a board and then experience a change, such as a job promotion that requires more of their time, preventing them from fully participating. Once a pattern of nonengagement occurs, it is best to have the conversation with the individual. They often feel stressed and conflicted about completing their board term. Explaining to them that this may not be a good time to volunteer on the board and the impact that their nonengagement is having may be enough to get them to resign. They may feel relief.

Formal individual board member assessments should begin with an annual self-assessment. Each member should complete the assessment as it relates to how well they meet the expectations of a board member.

Sample questions for that self-assessment are found in Table 9.1. It is best to provide a scale of 1 to 5 with a range of excellent to poor. Here the board will get insight into how the board member feels about their board service and how prepared they feel to conduct the business of the organization.

Table 9.1

Self-Evaluation Individual Board Member	Very Well	Good	Average	Fair	Poor
How well do I understand my board responsibilities					
I review the meeting materials in advance and feel prepared for the meetings					
Attendance is a priority for me, and I miss meetings and conference calls only rarely					
I understand our vision, mission, and strategic plan/goals					
I am a strong advocate for the organization and regularly promote it in my community					
I understand the role of the board versus staff and ensure that we stay on the policy and strategic level					
I feel involved and passionate about the organization and the board's work					

Key to a self-evaluation is the opportunity to provide comments or explanations for answers to each question. Open questions tend to provide more insight such as follows: What do you enjoy most about serving on the board? What would you recommend to improve your experience as a board member?

Next the board development committee and/or the board chair should conduct their evaluation of the board member. Typically, these cover how the board member is performing against expectations, including the following:

- Attendance
- Participation and thoughtful insights in meetings. Do they ask pertinent questions and use respectful language? Do they bring new ideas to meetings?
- Financial contributions as an individual and providing introductions to other donors

- Serving as a role model for other board members
- Recruiting other volunteers for events, committees, and board service
- Always being engaged and passionate about the organization
- Sharing their particular skill set that is the reason they were recruited to the board
- Staying informed about the programs offered by the organization and the issues faced by the organization
- Carrying out the duties of their office or other roles on committees such that the organization moves forward
- Keeping the interests of the organization ahead of any personal interests
- Reading board materials in advance of the meeting and being prepared asking any questions or raising issues in advance of the meeting
- Attending relevant conferences and educational sessions to improve their board and organizational expertise
- Showing the staff respect and support while holding them to high standards without directing their work
- Exhibiting high ethical standards and exercising their fiduciary responsibility putting the interests of the organization ahead of personal interests
- Serving as an advocate for the organization in their community of friends

Once the evaluation is done, the president or chair should meet either in person or over the phone with the board member to discuss the evaluation. The discussion should be a two-way dialogue gaining insight into how the board member feels about their service and experience. Any suggestions or concerns should be documented, and next steps should be identified for follow-up.

Board of Directors Self-Evaluation

The next step is for each board member to complete a self-evaluation from the perspective of the board as a whole functioning body. This is the opportunity to step back and consider how the board is performing its responsibilities. One approach would be for the board to discuss certain questions as a group. Table 9.2 provides sample questions to provoke a thoughtful discussion.

Another area to consider is the staff versus board relationship. Ask the staff in advance to provide feedback on the board. Areas to consider are communication and whether they feel respected. In particular, the executive director, who works most closely with the board, should be consulted for input on how they feel the board is functioning. Asking the executive director to share any frustrations or observations about areas for improvement will show that the board respects their role and opinions as well.

Table 9.2

Self-Evaluation for Board Group Discussion	Very Well	Good	Average	Fair	Poor
Does the board understand its responsibilities?					
Is there a clear organizational structure with roles defined?					
Is there a strategic plan with clear goals that serve as a basis for decision-making and budgets?					
Is the board focused on policy and planning versus operations?					
Does the board regularly receive reports on finances, program performance, and strategic goal progress?					
Does the board represent the membership and stakeholders of the organization taking positions that are consistent with the views of the membership and the mission of the organization?					
Is the board active among its stakeholders and visible in its community promoting the mission of the organization?					
Is progress toward the vision and strategic plan implementation regularly monitored?					
Does the board conduct an annual evaluation of the executive director and provide for continuous professional development?					
Does the board conduct training and team building to improve its functioning as a cohesive body?					
Does it ensure all points of view are heard and embrace diverse viewpoints?					
Does it regularly review all policies and update them as necessary?					
Are all necessary skill sets represented on the board as well as demographical characteristics of the members?					

Again time should be allocated for general comments about what is working well for the board, including its strengths and achievements for the year. An open discussion of what could have worked better and how things might be improved for the future should occur. The board may want to set some goals for the coming year related to how the board functions, such as 100% giving participation, 80% attendance at all meetings, or each board member participates in three local activities or events. Since the chair or president may be inclined to take certain opportunities for improvement as criticism of their leadership, it may be prudent to have the chair of the board development committee facilitate the discussion.

Board Knowledge Assessment

A board knowledge assessment indicates how well your board understands the key areas a board should possess an understanding of in order to exercise its fiduciary responsibility and be successful. Assessing the understanding of these areas identifies additional board training that may be needed as well as additional skill sets for recruiting new board members. These areas may vary based on the type of organization, so the following may not be all-inclusive.

Finance—How Well Do You Understand?

- The financial statements, including the statements of net assets and changes in net assets, the cash flow statement, the budget, the internal financial statements
- The liquidity needs of the organization and whether our bills are being paid on time and receivables collected on a timely basis
- The key drivers for financial success and stability for the organization
- Whether our key programs are financially stable, including the cost of staff time to administer them
- The audited or reviewed statements, including the footnotes
- The annual tax or information return
- The internal control environment
- Asset management—for example, how the organization is monitoring fixed assets as well as inventory, if any
- Financial policies and procedures

Human Resources—How Well Do You Understand?

- Hiring and termination policies and procedures
- Benefit arrangements and who is entitled to them

- Training programs particularly those to prevent harassment and minimize safety issues
- The process for employee evaluations and how pay and promotions are determined
- Succession planning for executive director and other key employees—how employees are being developed to move up in the organization

Risk Management—How Well Do You Understand?

- Insurance programs, including directors and officers insurance
- Organization continuity planning
- Member privacy
- Cybersecurity
- Key risks the organization faces
- Communication plan in the event of a major crisis/disaster/casualty
- Current and pending litigation: the importance of organization continuity— what happens if there is a disruption from a fire, storm, or power outage?
- Disaster planning and how the organization's operations would function in the event of a major event or even a short-term weather event forcing closure of operations
- The process that would be implemented in the event of the loss of the executive director due to death, illness, resignation, or termination

Board Governance and Operations—How Well Do You Understand?

- Board versus management duties.
- Management's view of the desired level of board engagement in certain tasks.
- Gaps where additional board engagement may be needed or additional training for key staff is required.
- How prepared board members are for the meetings. Are the board packets timely, relevant, and studied in advance? Are you getting the right level of information to make decisions and monitor the activities of the organization?
- Whether issues are identified prior to the meeting so that questions can be investigated prior to the meeting.
- The importance of attendance, participation, and open discussion.

Board Meetings and Training—How Well Do You Understand?

- Whether board meetings are efficient, productive, and focused on the proper strategic level of issues.

- The process for board review and approval of policies so that they are up-to-date and relevant.
- The development plan for board members and the board as a whole.
- How well the board is kept informed of best practices for nonprofit leadership and for the sector of the public it serves.
- The plan for full board education and training.
- Whether individual board members are encouraged to attend individual training.
- The new board members' orientation and whether it includes an introduction to the staff, the history of the organization, review of the financial status and programs offered, parliamentary procedures, and their responsibility as a board member. Are new board members encouraged to pursue additional training specific to the sector the organization serves?

Board Member Recruitment and Officer Succession Planning—How Well Do You Understand?

- The composition of your board. Is it diverse, and does it reflect the demographics of your stakeholders or membership?
- The plan for identifying and developing potential board members to ensure demographic diversity while replacing skill sets needed on the board.
- Board turnover—why do board members resign and what can we do to prevent it?
- The identification of potential board officers and the opportunities for learning the skills required to be a board officer.

Roles and Responsibilities of the Board for the Executive Director—How Well Do You Understand?

- The process for evaluating the organization's executive director on at least an annual basis
- The evaluation document and how it aligns with the strategic goals of the organization
- The goals for the executive director and suggestions for improvement in performance
- The resources provided to support the executive director
- How staff feels about the executive director and leadership they provide
- How the compensation of the executive director relates to the evaluation
- The discussion of the evaluation with the executive director and how it was perceived

- How satisfied the executive director is with their position, compensation, and the support received from the board
- The plan for the continued development of the executive director, including training, professional organization and meetings, and mentoring by board leadership
- Whether the duties are clearly defined and priorities are updated regularly to be consistent with the strategic plan
- Whether the executive director is encouraged to take the initiative to develop new opportunities for the growth of the organization
- Whether communication with the executive director is open and productive
- Whether there are opportunities for improvement in the relationship between the board and the executive director as well as the relationship between the executive director and their staff

Strategic Planning—How Well Do You Understand?

- The strategic plan—When was it developed? Who developed it? Does it need to be updated? Is it still relevant and realistic?
- Regular updates on the progress of implementing the strategic plan. Is it used as a guide for all decision-making and the setting of priorities?
- Whether it is reviewed annually in a board session focused exclusively on the strategic plan. Has the board considered an offsite retreat for the purpose of strategic planning?
- Whether the staff regularly consults the strategic plan as they establish their operational or tactical plans for the year. Do they provide input for the strategic plan?
- Whether the services or programs we provide continue to be needed by and relevant to those we serve.
- How well we are carrying out our mission.

Conducting an annual thorough board self-assessment of knowledge will assist with planning for the coming year. Evaluating where the board is lacking informs the board as to areas to focus on for training as well as areas that may require additional time in the board agenda. It is critical that all board members feel informed and comfortable in their board member roles.

Board Meeting Evaluation

At the conclusion of each board meeting, individual board members should complete a meeting evaluation. The evaluation can then be reviewed with the board chair and the executive director to assist in planning future meetings. Obtaining feedback from attendees assists in determining whether the board members find the meetings valuable and fulfilling. While Table 9.3 is a useful efficient tool for evaluating the meeting, providing sufficient space for comments is most helpful. On a scale of 1 to 5, with 5 being exceeds expectations and 1 being below expectations, ask the board meeting attendees to evaluate the criteria in Table 9.3.

Evaluating the individual board members, the board as a whole, and its knowledge base as well as the board meetings will help ensure a highly functioning, efficient board aligned to achieve the mission and strategic goals of the organization.

Table 9.3

Board Meeting Evaluation	1	2	3	4	5
The advance board materials were received with sufficient lead time for me to review them and get my questions answered					
The advance board materials provided the information I needed in sufficient detail					
The agenda was clear and delineated realistic time frames for adequate discussion					
The matters discussed in the meeting were strategic and appropriate for board-level decision-making					
We spent the right amount of time discussing each agenda item, providing each board member the opportunity to provide input					
Staff and officer reports were thorough and understandable					
Our discussions were aligned with our strategic plan					
I felt engaged and my opinion valued					
The educational topics were helpful					
I understand next steps and my follow-up assignments					
The meeting was conducted efficiently					
We accomplished what we needed to					
Additional Comments:					

Reality Check

The Successful Credit Union (SCU) was about to begin its planning for its spring board meeting and welcome new board and committee members. Several new members had already met with the president, the vice president of finance, and the vice president of administration for their orientation. They had been recruited by the nominating committee from a list of recommended members provided by board members. As SCU had expanded its membership, the nominating committee had tried to select new committee and board members who represented their membership and also possessed the skill sets such as knowledge of legal and finance matters that were needed. Additionally, it was important that the board include community leaders. SCU was expanding into new service offerings, and while a nonprofit established to serve those not served elsewhere in the financial services industry, it needed the business expertise and strategic thinking of a highly performing board. Business leaders were also recruited.

The new board chair was concerned about how the board and committee members were going to work together. There were only four meetings a year, and everyone needed to get up to speed quickly. The credit union industry was changing rapidly, and SCU was investing in people and technology to ensure they continued as leaders in the industry efficiently meeting the needs of their credit union members. The board chair had attended board chair training and heard about the tools offered for board evaluation. The board president had conducted personality testing of his management team and found it helpful in understanding how everyone might work together. He suggested having the DISC assessment done by each board member and key committee member.

A DISC consultant was engaged to conduct the testing and then come to the spring meeting to discuss the results. The testing was received well, and the results were informative. The consultant's discussion of how members with diverse personalities might work well together was particularly helpful. Understanding a fellow leader's approach to decision-making facilitated report preparation, discussion guidelines, and pre-meeting planning. Knowing that a fellow board member is going to approach a topic from a more introspective, more emotional view compared to another board member who may want to act quickly with just the facts helped each understand the type of information and discussion needed before being ready to make a decision.

One committee realized how it could use the behavioral styles to its advantage. Those members who were very analytical could be counted on to study the financial results and ask questions. Those members who were very persuasive presented recommendations to management and the board. The member who was both supportive and analytical was elected chair of the committee.

A knowledge self-assessment was conducted. Topics were identified for future meeting educational moments as well as for the annual fall retreat. New and continuing board and committee members were provided monthly with opportunities for relevant credit union industry meetings and training. One committee member took the initiative after attending a week of relevant industry training to pursue volunteer certification through additional training. To maintain her certification, she continues to stay current and share her knowledge of best practices with her committee.

The orientation process was expanded to be more helpful in understanding how SCU conducted operations including facility tours where new board members could meet departmental management.

The fall annual retreat included the latest trends in technology as well as a discussion of the risks facing SCU. It also provided updates on how well SCU was progressing on its mission of meeting the needs of the underserved as well as achieving its strategic goals and objectives. Time was included in the retreat for board and committee members to get to know each other as well as top management and their backgrounds.

All of these steps supported the development of individual board members as well as improving the effectiveness of the board. Increased confidence and improved relationships with each other as well as management led to improved engagement as board members felt they were able to contribute and enjoy their volunteer service to a growing organization.

CHAPTER TEN

What Should We Be Doing about Technology?

As a board member you may first hear about technology at your organization when you hear about the website going down or the database crashing or when you are notified your board materials will now be available on some software package you need to download. Then you may be surprised when the executive director includes a five- or six-figure capital project in the budget for a system upgrade and another large sum for hardware. A worst-case scenario is when you hear about the organization's technology problems when there is a cybersecurity breach. Then you may have to go into crisis mode, disclosing the breach to your stakeholders and the public. Board responsibilities include overseeing the development, implementation, and maintenance of the organization's information systems and, most important, the security over those systems.

Our stakeholders, the members, donors, and beneficiaries of our services, expect to be able to conduct "business" with the organization electronically. The way board members interact is often via new technology. How we communicate and publicize our organization must include electronic formats. Keep in mind, though, even the younger generations still enjoy and request paper formats, just in addition to electronic. Organizations are critically dependent on technology.

Some board members may be tech savvy from either having worked in the tech industry or having grown up in a technologically advanced environment (i.e., below the age of 60). They may have been involved in selecting and implementing technology at their companies. Others may have been dragged into this tech-dependent world kicking and screaming, clinging to their flip phones.

As board members address technology issues, they need to be cognizant of the wide diversity in knowledge and comfort with technology.

One approach may be to form a technology committee or task force of the board. The committee's responsibilities would include assessing the current state of technology, evaluating how it can support the strategic plan, and evaluating technology-related risks.

Cybersecurity—What Board Members Need to Ask?

In the current environment with technology entering every phase of our lives, the scariest facet is the risk to our data security. Board members have heard the horror stories such as the Target data breach that occurred using credentials stolen from its third-party heating ventilation air conditioning maintenance company. Board members need to ask what is being done to protect the organization and the data its members have trusted them with. Breaches in cybersecurity result from spyware, viruses, worms, ransom ware, and other evolving attacks. However, probably the most common way for information to be breached is through phishing. Phishing occurs when e-mails are sent from what appears to be a company or individual known to the recipient to get the recipient to reveal personal information such as passwords, social security numbers, and credit card numbers.

Board members need to understand common phishing techniques that continue to evolve with technology. According to the article "Cut Bait or Phish" by Emily Erickson, in *Credit Union Magazine*, December 2018, some of the most common phishing techniques include the following:

- Embedding links in e-mails or ads that redirect users to an unsecure website where they are prompted to provided passwords or other sensitive date
- Installing malware or causing unsuspecting users to install malware by downloading innocuous-looking attachments, for example, with the specific intention of accessing otherwise-protected information through loopholes in virus protection software
- Faking the identity of an e-mail sender to appear as a legitimate source and requesting sensitive personal or company information
- Impersonating personnel, like members of an IT department or a known third-party vendor, over the phone, in an attempt to obtain safeguarded data and information

According to the article, criminals continue to change their techniques, so one should not think one can recognize phishing e-mails. It is almost impossible to tell that an attachment is actually malware. Board members need to ask staff what security procedures are in place to provide safeguards. Key questions include the following:

- What antivirus and spam-blocking software is used, and how often is it updated?
- Are strong passwords required and changed regularly, and is there multifactor authentication?
- Is encryption required when transferring sensitive and confidential information?
- Are staff educated on best practices both for their personal and for work devices?
- Is the education done frequently enough to keep data security at the forefront of staff minds, and does it include the risks associated with social media and links therein?
- Are phishing tests run to determine who may need additional education?

Board member education about cybersecurity should also occur so that breaches do not inadvertently occur through a board member's carelessness. The board has the responsibility to ensure that cybersecurity is part of the control environment incorporated into training, risk assessment, and the organization's disaster recovery plan. Ask if there is a written plan for addressing unauthorized access (whether from internal or external sources) to sensitive data such as donor, employee, or member records. Are there safeguards to prevent the destruction of key data (whether accidental or intentional)? Are there controls and procedures to ensure the proper disposal of confidential information? These are just a few of the questions that should be asked of your organization and any third-party service providers.

Software to Facilitate the Effectiveness of Board Members

Great strides have been made in the development of software to improve the efficiency and effectiveness of board work. As more work is conducted virtually and remotely saving the costs of attending meetings in person, meeting software applications become part of conducting the business of the organization. Software such as Skype and Zoom allow video so participants can see each other, recording for future reference as well as documenting and screen sharing in real time. They are easy to set up, so meetings can occur immediately in just the time it takes to send a text or e-mail with the meeting ID number.

Board materials can now be made available electronically on a secure site with packages such as BoardPaq (boardpaq.com). Additional board communication and document sharing software such as Box (box.com), Freedcamp

(freedcamp.com), and Google Docs (docs.google.com) allow board members to review materials, edit them, ask questions, and share them securely. The host specifies who has access and can add to and delete from the files. Board members can access the materials at their convenience, and they are stored in the cloud and so do not need to be downloaded to review or edit.

The aforementioned are just a few frequently used software applications available to board members. Board members can find out more about board-related software by attending board training and industry conferences.

Considering a New System or Technology Upgrade

Once it is determined that new or upgraded systems are needed, the committee would work with staff to oversee the engagement of any consultants, review the needs assessment, review the requests for proposals (RFP) being sent to potential providers, identify potential service/equipment/software providers, review responses to the RFP, and meet with the finalists, including attending any necessary site visits. The level of involvement is a function of the skill set the staff possesses. If the organization is large enough to have an information systems department, the level of the task force involvement may be limited.

At a minimum, the board and/or its technology committee should ensure a thorough selection process and approve the budget for technology. The budget presented should include one-time investment in software/hardware purchases, consultant fees, and implementation costs. Additionally, the board should approve the ongoing costs, such as annual licensing fees, support fees, and upgrade fees, if any. In reviewing the process, the committee should counsel staff on allowing sufficient time for each step of the process. It always takes longer than is expected.

The Build versus Buy/Host versus Cloud Decisions

In the past, systems were developed either in-house or by consultants and were therefore totally customized to the organization. That required either internal systems development staff or consultants on retainer to make any future modifications, handle support issues, and train employees on the system. While such a system may have met the needs of the organization when initially implemented, it was quickly out of date in these times of rapid change. Each new initiative required either a modification or a new system, which may or may not interface with the main system. Unfortunately, many organizations face the decision of continued modification, requiring an investment in an antiquated system or starting over.

The proliferation of software applications and increased standardization of the platforms they work with have both improved affordability and reduced the need to develop systems internally. "Off-the-shelf" packages may not meet every need but often provide sufficient options in areas such as reporting that they can meet substantially all the needs. Missing functionality, if requested by enough users, may be incorporated into future upgrades to purchased software.

User groups often share thoughts on how to maximize the functionality of the software.

Add-on software applications are developed and can link directly to the main enterprise software via API (application programming interface), which is a software tool that allows one software application to input data, access features, and export data in another operating system. Because changes in technology happen so frequently, the build versus buy decision swings heavily in favor of buy or lease.

This brings us to the decision of host versus cloud. Hosting in simple terms means that the software system resides on the organization's hardware, typically referred to as a server. A server is a computer with enough capacity and speed to run the operating system. It physically is located in a dedicated data center either on or off premises. Generators may be needed to keep the data center running in the event of a power outage. A backup center in another location is needed in the event of a local disaster such as fire or hurricane. Contractors or internal personnel are needed to monitor and maintain the data center servers. There are benefits to hosting, including more control over security. Hosting can be done on a third-party or external service provider's infrastructure. The service provider provides agreed-on services for a fee, and normally you have dedicated servers at the provider's data center. They provide appropriate security and maintenance.

The next option, which has become popular, is cloud hosting. According to Techopedia, "Cloud Hosting is the procurement of computing resources from a cloud computing provider or facility to host data, services and/or solutions." The organization uses virtual hardware on a network for all of its computing needs. The cloud hosting provider charges a fee to deliver the software to each of its users on demand. Typically, a monthly fee that is based on the number of users of the system is required. It provides maximum flexibility since the capacity grows as the organization needs it. Users from different organizations use the same cloud hosting service protected with access controls. An additional advantage is that cloud service providers often maintain higher levels of cybersecurity. Their future is dependent on being able to provide the assurance of security. Security is the most critical attribute to be evaluated when considering a third-party hosting or cloud hosting arrangement.

If board members attend conferences for their type of organization, technology providers will probably be there promoting their newest systems and services. It is easy to become overwhelmed, especially if you consider "Tech" a four-letter word.

What Do We Have Now?

As a board member you may want to ask the staff for a listing of the current software applications and operating platforms. The operating platform means that the systems were designed to run a certain way, so they all work together. The operating system or platform supports basic functions such as scheduling tasks and managing the hardware and software resources, including memory. Request that the list include when the software was last updated and whether automatic updates occur. Virus protection software, for example, needs to be updated frequently.

Having the list is the first step in performing a risk assessment of your systems. Outside expertise is often required to perform a system risk assessment. If your organization is large enough to have an internal audit department, expertise in evaluating system controls is a critical skill set. External audit firms possess expertise in this area and should be conducting an evaluation in conjunction with determining the adequacy of controls to ensure the accuracy of financial statements. The assessment should also include an assessment of hardware needs. How often are desktop and laptop computers replaced? What is the security to protect against access and theft? What training is conducted around cybersecurity? What control risks are present?

The board is not responsible for conducting the systems inventory but is responsible for ensuring a risk assessment is performed and understanding that risk assessment.

What Do We Need?

The next step is a needs assessment. Limitations of the current systems may be restricting our ability to fulfill our mission. What do our stakeholders expect and need? What is consuming significant staff time that could be automated? Manual steps increase the risk of error. Are there upgrades to existing systems that could be implemented immediately? Are we maximizing the current capabilities of our systems? Consider critical needs versus nice-to-have "latest and greatest."

Part of the strategic plan implementation should be an evaluation of what technology is needed to support new and continuing initiatives. Changes in regulatory requirements may also precipitate the need for new hardware and software as well as control procedures around them. For example, the European Union's new General Data Protection Regulation, which governs data privacy, has many organizations with members, donors, or beneficiaries in Europe scrambling to understand the new requirements.

What Is GDPR?

The General Data Protection Regulation requires any organization offering goods and services to European Union (EU) residents to comply with certain privacy and disclosure requirements. For example, if the organization uses a cookie, a member subject to the EU GDPR needs to be notified and has to explicitly consent to having it used. EU residents must specifically consent to the processing and sharing of their data, and opting out is not sufficient. Consult an expert if your organization has members in the EU.

The needs assessment should be thorough and well documented. If a decision is made to implement a new system, the needs assessment will be the basis for the system design/selection. Often a consultant with system needs assessment expertise should be engaged. Each department should be interviewed to determine its system needs and priorities. An interdepartmental task force could be convened to prevent a silo approach and develop improved communication.

Again, it is not the board's responsibility to conduct the needs assessment but rather to ensure it is conducted thoroughly and documented. Some organizations may require the assistance of a board member with systems expertise in the needs assessment. They may be an integral part of the task force conducting the needs assessment, but it is the staff who will have the ultimate responsibility and input.

In addition to staff and board members, a thorough needs assessment should include interviews with members, volunteer leadership, donors, and those we serve. What frustrates them about the organization's website and services conducted electronically? A donor, hearing about how a new system can improve how the organization delivers services may want to help fund the system. When performing the needs analysis, it is best to categorize needs by function with additional sections for areas of technology that impact multiple functions. The following are sample categories for completing the needs analysis:

- Membership services
- Fund-raising or development
- Program services
- Events/training
- Finance
- Personnel/human resources/payroll

- Board services
- Investment management/endowment management
- Administration
- Data security
- Fixed assets and/or collections
- Mobile/web services

This is a sample list to help organize the needs analysis. Some of these areas may have multiple functions/departments within them. Each functional area should have the opportunity to list its system requirements, including the requirements to conduct its responsibilities and what would be welcome functionality (nice to have but not a priority). For the later, an explanation of the impact of the additional functionality should be documented. Encourage the staff to think into the future of the organization and consider the long-term strategic plan.

What Are Our Options?

Identifying options to meet the needs requires patience and investigation. Contacting other similar organizations that may have recently implemented new systems can be helpful. Prospective providers are normally happy to provide contacts of other organizations that have recently implemented their systems. Attending conferences where potential providers exhibit or speak can be helpful. Current providers do not want to lose you and often will provide low- or no-cost feature upgrades to keep you. Checking the websites of similar organizations may also provide ideas on provider options. Because consultants specialize in specific sectors of nonprofit organizations, they are often a great resource for identifying options. Engaging a consultant at this point is another option. Be sure they do not have relationships/expertise with only one system provider.

Historically, the term "enterprise system" meant an expensive, one-stop system that would do everything for an organization from membership to fund-raising to finance to personnel. Current trends are toward a primary system for the organization with applications for fund-raising and/or finance that link seamlessly to the primary system. For example, a membership organization may look for an association membership management system that provides the searchable databases and event management functionality it needs but links via an API (see earlier) to the finance and website management system.

As more of our stakeholders use their cellphones as their computers, remember to ensure that the system is "mobile device friendly." The goal is to deliver our services and message across whatever devices our stakeholders utilize.

Requests for Proposal

After identifying possible service providers and documenting the needs or system requirements, an RFP should be drafted. Components of an RFP may include the following:

- Description of the organization, including its expected growth plans
- Financial summary data
- Selection process and time frame for responses, evaluation, interviews, final selection, and system implementation
- Activity volume and nature of transactions, including number of employees, sales transaction volume and average sales ticket, number of members, number and nature of events and training sessions, and so on
- Current operating platform and any system integration issues
- Listing of systems expected to remain in place
- Detailed needs analysis as an attachment
- Contact information for persons available to answer questions or to request additional information
- Listing of items to be included in the response and method to provide response (mail and/or electronic):
  - Experience with similar organizations
  - Comparison of system functionality with needs assessment
  - Support availability
  - Frequency of upgrades
  - Primary contacts, including who will serve on the implementation team as well as conduct training
  - APIs and software applications recommended to achieve functionality, including experience with other installations
  - Operating system platform
  - References
  - User groups
  - Hardware requirements if not remotely hosted
  - Costs, including ongoing support, training, license, and upgrade fees

The RFP must provide sufficient information for the responder to understand your needs and the organization. Consultants can assist with the drafting of the RFP, and board members may be able to provide examples from their companies. Once a potential system provider receives the RFP, they may want to make a site visit and ask questions to further clarify expectations and needs. Often conference calls will suffice for getting questions answered.

How Do We Evaluate Our Options?

Once the responses to the RFPs are received, the task force should individually review them. Additional clarification may be needed. Throughout the process the decision-making team obtains additional data points, which may raise additional questions. It is appropriate to contact the RFP responders and ask additional questions. For example, one software may have a functionality that the team did not previously consider and then needs to determine if the other applications incorporate the same functionality.

Often it is helpful to rank the responses against the needs analysis on a numerical basis. Table 10.1 provides a simple example of a ranking for one sample membership organization. Each team member evaluating the responses should do the ranking. The results can then be compiled by the staff and used for a team discussion. Again additional clarification and conversations with the potential providers may be required.

Table 10.1 shows a method for ranking that weights the requirements as to importance and computes a weighted score for each section, which is then totaled so that the group can compare alternative vendors.

At this point the team should be able to narrow down the potential suppliers to a maximum of three. Those three finalists may be invited to make an oral presentation and demonstrate their software/system. For smaller organizations, this may be accomplished through a web-based conference call. For larger organizations making a larger investment, a visit by the team to the site is suggested. You want to get a sense as to how well you will work together, and a face-to-face meeting provides a better indication. At the conclusion of each presentation, allow sufficient time for the team to discuss impressions and concerns about what was presented. The ranking may be modified. Differing interpretations of what was heard should be clarified.

Team or task force members may be assigned references to call or even visit to see how the systems perform for other organizations. Not-for-profit organizations are different, and each has its own culture and information needs that need to be taken into consideration. The results of the calls and visits should then be reported back to the entire task force.

Costs and resource needs will be a limiting factor for most organizations. Therefore, it is important to prioritize the needs. While sometimes difficult, a return-on-investment analysis should be performed once costs are determined. An improved database system may result in more targeted fundraising, resulting in increased donations. An improved electronic application

Table 10.1

SAMPLE NEEDS ASSESSMENT RANKING CHART

Vendor:

Product:

Date Reviewed: TOTAL SCORE   40.2

Requirements	Weight	Feature support		Weighted Score	Justification
		Total			
Mobile app	**H = 100%**	Total	9	**9**	
Do they have a mobile app for the user base		M	2		
Is there a mobile app for the administration		L	1		
Is it possible to have separate apps for affiliates		L	1		
Directory management (for members and spouses)		L	1		
Social networking		L	1		
Add notes about members		L	1		
Message members		M	2		
Functionality—architecture	**H**	Total	15	**15**	
Open API architecture		H	3		
Cloud based		M	2		
Compatible with existing systems		H	3		
Scalable and flexible platform		M	2		
Customizable fields		H	3		
Searchable database		M	2		

(Continued)

Table 10.1 (Continued)

SAMPLE NEEDS ASSESSMENT RANKING CHART

Event management	L = 40%	Total	16	6.4
Agenda	H	3		
Ability to provide feedback	L	1		
Attendees with ability to make notes on contacts and opportunities	M	2		
Hotel information	M	2		
Logistics	M	2		
Payment features for events, dinners, outings	M	2		
Signup features for side events, with ability for user to change	M	2		
Foundational accounting	**M = 70%**	Total	14	9.8
Fund-raising	H	3		
Open API	L	1		
Automated batching	M	2		
Manage finances across multiple revenue sources	M	2		
Financial reporting, chart of accounts	M	2		
Integrates well with finance software	M	2		
Ability to handle multiple currencies	M	2		

(Developed with Dan L. Ciprari, technology executive and Society of International Business Fellows board member) process may result in more members and more dues revenue. Each of these is an example of how a system may pay for itself in as little as a few years. Then there is the improved program delivery impact of a new system. That is harder to quantify but critical to the mission of the organization.

Making the Decision

Once the task force agrees on a recommendation, a presentation should be made to the ultimate decision maker. Depending on the size of the investment, the decision maker may be the executive director of the organization. Sharing the process with the key staff not on the task force is critical to the success of implementation since you will have more buy-in. The more everyone understands the positive impact of the new system, the more excited they will be to adopt it, learn about its capabilities, and maximize its functionality.

More significant changes and investments should be brought to the board. There may have been board oversight and participation in the process. The board representatives on the task force should regularly update the board on the process. A demonstration of the capabilities of the new system and how it will help the organization achieve its strategic priorities should be presented. The financial impact on the organization should be delineated and may require board approval before proceeding.

It is often difficult to raise funds specifically for new systems and infrastructure. Board members will need to explore where the funds will come from, both for any initial investment and for the ongoing annual incremental costs. Boards may be surprised by the costs of new systems, especially if funding is tight. They must be comfortable as to whether the organization has the financial capacity to take on any such major project. Staff may be disappointed if the board requests a less-expensive alternative such as modifying existing systems. Hopefully, all options must be considered during the process such that the board is comfortable with the recommendation, funding is appropriated, and implementation can begin.

Reality Check

A new treasurer of the board of the society had just been elected. The executive director (ED) suggested that she visit headquarters, review the financials, and gain an understanding of some of the financial issues that the ED needed help with. Immediately she noticed that the financial software did not support nonprofit fund accounting. It required substantial staff and ED time to enter journal entries to reflect the proper accounting for restricted funds and their transactions. The audit was made more difficult and costlier as the conversion was required to fund accounting.

Shortly thereafter, the board embarked on a strategic planning process. It became clear that new systems were needed in order to implement the initiatives included in the strategic plan. The board chair appointed a task force of board members, staff, and key volunteers to investigate a new, enterprise-wide system, including a new finance system and new event software.

Because the society had affiliated organizations around the world, and a key strategic initiative was increased networking among members around the world, the system had to meet the needs of the affiliated networks as well. An added time pressure was that the affiliated networks were conducting their own search for a new system and had already engaged one of their members to start developing a new system.

Because this was an organization of entrepreneurial executives, many of whom were from leading technology companies, the task force contained some of the latest thinking in technology. The strategic plan emphasized that the organization needed to attract younger members, and that meant a strong need for mobile applications for the members.

The task force began by obtaining an understanding of the current system and identifying the issues with the existing system. The chair of the task force asked the liaisons for each of the international affiliates to discuss their needs with the affiliate board chairs and staff. The needs assessment had begun.

The task force chair set up an office messaging application, Slack, and invited the task force to join the group. Each member could then add to the discussion with information they obtained and ask questions. Meetings were scheduled using the application on a weekly basis. Staff and board members began providing names of potential software applications. Because the society was already using purchased software hosted by a third party and because there was no information technology staff, building its own system was not an option. That had been attempted when a member offered to build a customized system at a minimal cost, and three years later there had been little progress. As they say, you get what you pay for.

Based on their organizational roles and expertise, each task force member was assigned responsibility for conducting interviews and documenting the needs assessment for a particular functional area. For example, the treasurer was assigned responsibility for the finance area. The event management staff person was assigned responsibility for the events area. Another task force member had recently attended a conference where they used some event software and was impressed with it. He suggested with the ED's agreement trying it at the next conference of the society. The member whose company was involved with the latest in mobile applications was responsible for researching the latest in that area.

Because the society was a membership organization and the primary system needed to be an association management system, the task force focused on the companies providing association management systems. One of the first calls was to the existing supplier. It had recently merged with several other association management system software development companies and so now had a wide range of offerings to meet the needs of small-to-large organizations.

On that first conference call, on expressing concerns about the software application currently in use, a retention specialist was assigned. All of a sudden, the society was being offered upgrades for free on its existing software. Because the society had not developed a relationship with its provider and did not participate in the user group, it was unaware of the full functionality of its current system.

As the task force members spoke with other potential suppliers, they learned about additional functionality that would improve the way the organization worked with its members. That was added to the needs assessment. It became apparent that none of the association management systems included finance and development systems but were able to link with such systems via an API. The selection of those systems was postponed until after the selection of the association management system.

Preliminary calls were held with each potential provider. Based on those calls, functionality was compared with the needs assessment on a preliminary basis. The task force determined cost range and the target organization size for each package. Keeping in mind the expected growth of the society, the needs of the affiliates, and the budget restrictions, as well as the detailed comparison with the needs assessment, the number of potential suppliers was narrowed to three. Each of the three was sent the needs assessment document in a request for information document. No formal RFP was drafted, but the request for information included background information on the society, contact information, requests for references, and a listing of other organizations using their software.

Due to emphasis on mobile functionality, a significant amount of research was conducted on whether to utilize an add-on software or utilize the functionality within the packages being considered. Interestingly the same provider for mobile functionality kept coming up, and it appeared to work well with all the systems under consideration. But it was expensive, and the treasurer was concerned about funding it.

Detailed interviews of the final three were conducted. At the conclusion of each interview, the task force was asked to rank the system's functionality compared to the needs assessment. Then the group discussed the ranking. The field was narrowed to two, an upgraded version of the current system with a new mobile application and a more sophisticated new system.

Meanwhile the chair of the task force was providing monthly updates to the executive committee of the board. At one board meeting the status as well as a brief demonstration of the final two systems was presented. The board asked for cost estimates, and a range was provided.

References were checked, and responses were documented in Slack for all to review. More conversations were held with the international affiliates, who were concerned about costs. Ultimately the task force decided the most cost-effective and efficient approach was to upgrade the current system and link with a new mobile application. The board was presented the recommendation and approved it, subject to finding additional funding. Potential donors were identified, reserves were appropriated, and the project is beginning implementation. Due to the well-documented thorough process, which took six months, the entire staff and board are excited about and committed to the project and the impact it will have on achieving the future plans for the society.

CHAPTER ELEVEN

Engaging Volunteers

We are volunteers in our board roles for our nonprofit organization, and we probably have many volunteers whom we need to engage, nurture, and develop. Some may be our successor on the board. Some may be that next major donor. Some may become close friends for life. What most of us know is that without a strong volunteer network, our organization cannot accomplish its mission and deliver its programs.

In their book *The New Breed: Understanding and Equipping the 21st Century Volunteer* (published 2007 by Group), authors Jonathan McKee and Thomas W. McKee identify three roles for working with today's volunteers:

Volunteer recruiter—must "understand how to recruit the new breed of volunteer who is 'cause' driven"

Volunteer manager—must "understand how to empower the new breed of volunteer, who wants to be led instead of managed"

Volunteer leader—must "understand how to establish the power and passion of your volunteer team"

This book has a wealth of information on how to interact with today's volunteers and will be referred to throughout this chapter as *The New Breed*.

Some nonprofit organizations require large groups of volunteers for large-scale events. All require small groups such as boards and committees. It is important to be aware of the dynamics occurring within such small groups since it will affect the productivity of the organization. Leadership must understand the value of the committee as a way of accomplishing tasks and must have a clear understanding of mutual roles and responsibilities.

Committees

Volunteer committees should be a major asset to the board. They can tackle research and evaluation of proposed policies as well as execute short-term tasks. Because they are focused on a specific area of responsibility, they can take the time to acquire necessary data to make an informed recommendation. They may have specific experience, interest, training, and skills so that they are more qualified for evaluating and analyzing an issue. Committees allow the organization to train future leadership while assessing the individual's commitment to the organization and their leadership strengths. Smaller groups tend to be excellent at problem-solving because of their small size and informal nature.

Boards must ensure all volunteer committees are aligned with the mission and purpose of the organization. They should formally communicate the responsibilities delegated to the committee and set the deadlines and expectations. A board liaison to the committee can monitor progress, ensure priorities of the committee are consistent with priorities of the board, and report back to the board on the committee's progress. Paid staff should also be assigned to support the committee.

The board chair is normally responsible for appointing volunteers to committees but may be supported by staff and other board members in identifying those with the skills and interest in the area of the committee's responsibility. Just as diversity is important for a board, it is also important for a committee in order to ensure a variety of points of view. Divergent thinking is better for considering all alternatives. If a group is too cohesive or so comfortable working with one another, the emphasis may be on getting to a unanimous decision instead of thoroughly considering all options. Volunteers may be appointed because they have access to information and resources. They may represent varying agencies or affiliated groups, be from different geographic areas, and represent diverse demographics. A good blend of experienced and new volunteers aids in training. Most of all, though, they should be passionate about the organization and its mission and interested in the area of responsibility.

A subjective consideration is how well they work with others. Will they try to dominate the discussion and force their opinions on the other volunteers? Do they have their own agenda that will prevent them from considering diverse points of view? Are they willing to put their personal needs aside for the needs of the organization? Are they open to new ideas or locked into the "this is how we have always done it" mentality? Do they show respect to others? Are they good listeners and communicators? Are they willing to do whatever is necessary to accomplish the task? There is only one committee chair. Are they willing to accept direction and coaching from the committee chair? How flexible are they, and how do they handle inevitable changes in plans? Do they have the time necessary to fulfill the responsibilities? Are they willing to be held accountable?

The chair may not know the answers to each of these questions but should check with others who previously volunteered with the individual (i.e., check references when possible). It is difficult to have conversations about accountability with volunteers and so much better to prevent a problem than deal with it later. Interviewing a potential volunteer is an effective way of judging interest in serving and assessing why the volunteer is interested in serving. You are offering the opportunity to join others in accomplishing something. They should want what you are offering—for their own personal interest and development. If they are volunteering only because their friend or employer talked them into it, they may not make committee service a priority.

Recruiting Volunteers

We all hear that people are busier these days and just don't have time to volunteer, or the older volunteers comment that they have done "their time" and suggest that it is time for younger people to step up. Why do some organizations have many volunteers, while others never seem to have enough?

In *The New Breed*, the authors discuss societal shifts that impact today's volunteers. The first shift they discuss is the shift away from a nuclear family with a stay-at-home mother and retired grandparents, who had time to be those school volunteers. Now many women work outside the home and may be single parents with many additional responsibilities. The second shift they discuss is a move toward isolation with many social media friends but fewer close confidants. They are "less likely to be involved in groups that volunteer." However, with the increase in major disasters, there has been an increase in the number of people volunteering as individuals versus group volunteering done in the past according to *The New Breed*.

The third shift described in *The New Breed* is a requirement for flexibility—"from rigid scheduling to volunteer availability." Volunteers want to work on their own schedules. Organizations that are successful at recruiting volunteers ask volunteers how they want to be involved rather than trying to fill set schedules. The volunteer recruiter should listen more than talk asking a volunteer to drop by and share their thoughts. Do not demand a commitment to a schedule—ask for a commitment to the organization.

The fourth shift discussed in *The New Breed* is the younger generation of those born after 1981, referred to often as "millennials," who don't want to be micromanaged and who want to volunteer when and where they want. As volunteer recruiters, we need to figure out how to reach them and create the right environment to meet their needs.

According to *The New Breed*, "The new breed of volunteer wants to call the shots. These volunteers want to be asked what they see as the needs in the organization and how they can help accomplish the mission." They want to know that what they are doing will make a difference.

A successful volunteer recruiter will take the time to build a relationship and get to know the potential volunteer before asking them to sign up. Listening is critical. Consider giving them a tour of the operation. Obtain an understanding of their level of knowledge about the organization.

Start by asking them to get involved in small one-time tasks. After or during that volunteer experience, solicit their feedback. This also gives you the opportunity to learn their skill sets and consider where they might fit in best. Today's volunteer is going to be much more willing to help with a short-term task than make a long-term commitment. However, a good experience with a short-term project often leads to a longer commitment.

Younger and, more and more, older volunteers are tech savvy. They respond well to social media recruitment. Many organizations have effectively developed volunteer portals to encourage volunteers to learn more about volunteer opportunities as well as register for those opportunities. Providing position descriptions and expectations on the volunteer portal allows prospective volunteers to pursue the information on their schedule.

Setting expectations prior to gaining a commitment prevents surprises and an unhappy volunteer later. While you do not want to scare them off, they may want to select a different opportunity with less time requirements. Remember high volunteer turnover is expensive in time and money. A short presentation outlining volunteer expectations is all that is needed at this point for recruiting for short-term projects. For larger volunteer leadership roles, position descriptions should be developed and shared in advance.

In *The New Breed*, the authors also discuss recruiting methods. Merely posting an announcement or advertisement for volunteers to sign up is not effective. Volunteers want a personalized ask. The volunteer portal discussed earlier is just an introductory step. What matters is the follow-up conversations. This approach requires a team approach to recruiting. That is why every board member should understand that they have a role in recruiting volunteers and not just to be future board members. Current volunteers can be your best recruiters by sharing their experiences and why they enjoy volunteering so much. Passion is contagious, so testimonials are effective.

As a board member, meet the staff person responsible for volunteer recruitment and engagement. Are they volunteer focused? Do they understand the importance of "courting" volunteers and then showing them appreciation and respect?

When recruiting volunteers, keep in mind the life stage of the potential volunteer. Consider baby boomers (generally born between 1946 and 1964). They are just entering the retirement life stage, worked hard professionally, and may be looking for volunteer opportunities to ease adjustment into retirement. They have been health conscious and have many years ahead of them to volunteer. As stated in *The New Breed*, "Boomers want to be recruited to use a lifetime of experience to help you accomplish your vision." This generation is not afraid to commit if they see a personal benefit and are passionate about the mission. They do travel more, and there are the grandchildren in another state, so they need flexibility.

The next largest population potential for recruiting volunteers is the millennials, born between 1981 and 1994. They are currently the same-size population segment as baby boomers. They are service oriented, and many had service-hour requirements in high school and college. They grew up in the information age and are used to getting instant answers—patience may not be their virtue. They are quick learners and are motivated by being given more responsibility. They are multitaskers and active in social media. They process information quickly and want to see the impact they are making just as quickly. Diversity is valued, and they readily accept our international society. They want to get to know and develop relationships with those around the world—again with the use of technology. They grab on to a cause and run with it. Because millennials change jobs much more frequently than boomers, one benefit they see in volunteering is to network with potential employers. They listen to and follow the lead of their friends, so traditional recruiting is ineffective. For them, the most effective recruiter is your current volunteers in their peer group.

Engaging the Work of Volunteers

As discussed in the previous section, one of the most significant impacts on managing volunteers is the Internet. The Internet allows leaders to recruit and manage volunteers around the world in real time. These may be "virtual" volunteers that accomplish all their tasks via the Internet. Time is a valuable commodity for today's volunteers. If they can meet remotely, that saves them time. They expect efficient, well-run activities and meetings.

Remember the old adage, "When you want something done, ask a busy person." It is still true, but now expectations of those busy people have changed. They may want to be asked to be in charge of something that uses their skills.

Today many volunteers are professionals and expect to be treated like professionals. They often come from a structured business environment and expect that environment to continue as they volunteer with a nonprofit. They apply their business knowledge to their volunteer experience. Hence, the following steps outlined are consistent with their work world.

The first step in managing the work of volunteers is planning their work. Goals and objectives based on the board's priorities and needs for the committee should be delineated and explained to the committee. The planning may then involve the committee members as they consider how best to carry out the responsibilities delineated to them. They may need to go back to the board to secure approval for the plan. They should plan for frequency and method of meetings (in person, conference call, etc.). They should develop a timeline for components of the assigned tasks, allowing sufficient time to gather data. They should plan for their resource needs, including a financial budget and human resource needs (both staff and additional volunteer needs). They should develop checkpoints for measuring progress.

Once they have their plan, the group members can then organize itself to accomplish the plan. They may assign subgroups particular tasks. They may ask staff to gather, analyze, and present data. They should establish the sequence of activities or tasks. The timing of major steps should be organized to prevent delays if one step cannot be accomplished before another is completed. Always consider what could go wrong and its risk of happening. Plan for how delays or a shortage of resources may impact plan implementation. Organize communication of progress and marketing, if applicable, for participation and engaging additional volunteers/attendees. The chair should set the agenda for each meeting and ask an attendee to take minutes. Depending on the formality of the meetings, the chair will also educate volunteers about the rules of order for the meetings.

The next key component to managing volunteers is directing and monitoring progress as well as the quality of the work being performed by volunteers. The chair and board liaison may want to solicit feedback from the volunteers. Do they feel their efforts are appreciated? Do they feel they are accomplishing something? Are they enjoying their volunteer service? Often organizations wait until the end of the event or task before asking, but it is more effective to ask throughout the year. Problems with leadership and volunteers should be addressed early, preventing larger problems or unhappy volunteers. Supervising also means holding volunteers accountable. If the plan indicated that a particular volunteer should have gotten signed contracts for event entertainment by now, find out if they have them or what the status is. If press releases should have been drafted by now, where are they? Who is going to review them for quality and accuracy?

Boards should expect regular reports on progress of the committee. Boards may want to distribute a standard template for status updates. Reports should be distributed electronically or added to file storage software such as Google Docs or Microsoft SharePoint. That will permit real-time access and updating. Compliance with policies should be monitored. Are volunteers complying with budgetary restrictions and internal controls? If a volunteer collects cash donations, do they maintain a receipt book with the needed donor information and provide a receipt to the donor? If a volunteer expends personal funds expecting to be reimbursed by the organization, do they keep copies of purchase receipts, and are they aware of the amount budgeted for the expenditure?

Volunteers may get carried away wanting their event or activity to be the most outstanding ever with the best decorations or caterer. They may lose focus on the reason for the event in their desire to throw the best party ever. The goal is to raise the most funds or promote the organization and is probably not to have the most elegantly decorated venue. Educating and reminding volunteers of the purpose of the activity and how much is remaining of their budget must be done at every meeting. Unfortunately, the chair may have to inform a volunteer that they will not be reimbursed for expenditures above their budget. Again, regular monitoring of financial commitments can prevent such an embarrassing situation.

Staff are often in the best position to monitor progress. If a volunteer has "gone dark" and is not keeping everyone informed of their progress, there may be a problem. Staff can contact the volunteer and obtain an understanding of the situation. Staff are experienced in managing volunteers and know when to be supportive and compassionate and when a lack of action jeopardizes the accomplishment of the goals. Ideally, every key volunteer role has a backup volunteer. Committees and subcommittees should have vice chairs who can assist if the chair is unavailable.

Staff are also responsible for directing the day-to-day activities of the volunteer committees. They understand that while volunteers may be assigned responsibility, the event or activity must go on with or without a particular volunteer. They know when to step in, counsel a volunteer, and advise the responsible board member of issues. They are the continuity for the activities of the organization. Volunteers come and go, but the staff continue. Unless they are new to the organization, they have the best understanding of risks and what needs to be done when.

Just as boards need to perform self and organizational evaluations, volunteer committee members should participate in evaluating the work of the organization and the committee's effectiveness. The committee chair often establishes criteria for measuring effectiveness with the assistance of staff. The chair leads the evaluation process and requests data such as surveys to assist in the review process. What worked well for the committee? What did not work well, and what are the suggestions for improvement? Confidentially, which volunteers should be asked to return or accept more responsibility? One-on-one interviews of key volunteers may be conducted to determine if their expectations were met and their interest in continuing in the future. Goals and objectives for the future should be documented.

Role of Volunteer Committee Chair

The volunteer committee chair has the most impact on managing the volunteers and also has the most impact on their experience. The committee chair should possess outstanding people skills in addition to leadership skills. The chair must understand the priorities of the board and how the committee's work is critical to the success of the organization. The chair interprets the board priorities for the committee. The chair builds their team and develops loyalty among the team. The chair understands the importance of building relationships among the volunteers. Helping cultivate friendships by building in social time works well. The chair focuses on the "we," not the "I." While the chair may have to be forceful at times, generally leading by example and working with the committee accomplishes the goals more effectively. The chair should help each committee member be successful.

The chair welcomes and leads the orientation for new volunteers, possibly arranging for new volunteer mentoring by experienced volunteers. The chair guides the committee through its plan and day-to-day activities, delegating responsibilities to individual members or subgroups. The chair leads the committee through the budget and other resource planning process. The chair works closely with the board liaison and staff liaison to ensure the committee stays on track. When conflict or disagreements arise, the chair ensures all points of view are heard and that members understand conflict is part of healthy decision-making and not personal. When there are volunteer performance issues, the chair has the difficult task of meeting with the volunteer and discussing steps for improvement.

The chair normally communicates with the board and the other stakeholders. Having the committee review the draft reports prior to sending ensures accuracy and furthers engagement. The chair must be extremely organized and able to lead meetings, efficiently sticking to the agenda. The chair must understand parliamentary procedure. The chair is responsible for keeping the committee on task and on the timeline. As primary staff contact, the chair models a respectful approach to the staff and clarifies volunteer versus staff responsibilities. The chair keeps volunteers out of the day-to-day operations that are staff functions.

The chair monitors volunteer workloads and reallocates volunteer resources as necessary. The chair also breaks large projects down into manageable tasks. The chair is also the "cheerleader" of the group, making the volunteer's work as enjoyable as possible. No matter the problems the chair may be aware of, they must always keep a positive attitude. The chair works with staff and the committee to anticipate problems and develop solutions. Keeping the goal in sight also helps motivate the volunteer.

Considering today's volunteers, the chair's greatest challenge may be in figuring out how to empower the volunteers to make decisions. They need the information to make informed decisions, but then they need to feel in control of the situation in order to execute the task. Remember they want to be led, not controlled. Getting volunteers to develop potential solutions prior to bringing the problem to you is important. You may be comfortable at first with delegating certain tasks but keeping all final decisions as your responsibility. Once the chair is comfortable with the volunteer's decision-making process, the chair can empower the volunteer to make the decision. Once you empower them, you must be careful not to criticize but to coach as to how the process could be improved. Meeting on a regular basis with the empowered volunteer ensures alignment of goals and good communication.

Thanking volunteers and staff frequently and recognizing significant contributions are also key to motivating both volunteers and staff. A strong chair is a good listener and always available to their volunteer and staff team. A strong chair keeps their thoughts to themselves until all others have spoken in order to not unduly influence decision-making.

Volunteer Motivation, Recognition, and Celebration

Volunteers, whether boomers or millennials, want to have fun. They enjoy team-building activities, fun training retreats, and celebrations of success. They want to be part of a winning team but for a cause. Younger volunteers welcome the opportunity to build relationships with older, more experienced volunteers. Provide such opportunities with fun activities that allow everyone to get to know one another. And then the free food factor is always a motivation.

It is easy to get so involved in the day-to-day issues and forget to make the volunteer experience fun. Volunteers won't keep coming if their tasks are all work and no play. Leaders must exhibit a sense of humor and know when to interject humor and fun into activities from meetings to training. We all need to laugh at ourselves sometimes, and sharing a faux pas makes a leader more human and approachable.

We can't motivate our volunteers with pay, so how do we motivate volunteers? First ask them why they stay involved. It might be a personal need such as for friendship or their belief in the cause. Maybe a relative was affected by an illness your organization does research for. Being passionate about the cause yields the highest level of commitment.

Volunteers want feedback and recognition when they deserve it. Maybe they don't need praise (some volunteers do), but a recognition of the effort invested in the task is absolutely necessary. Otherwise, how does a volunteer know that what they did was of value to the organization? Pubic recognition among peers at a board or committee meeting and in the newsletter can be a significant factor in getting volunteers to go above and beyond.

Families often have a great deal of influence on how engaged a volunteer is. They also impact the level of financial giving. Remember to thank and recognize the family of the volunteer along with the volunteer.

In today's electronic media world, handwritten notes stand out as special recognition. We all need encouragement and a reminder that what we are doing is making a difference.

Volunteers are also motivated by special privileges. Such privileges need to be unique and of interest to the volunteer, not just an event T-shirt. Golf tournament volunteers might receive a round of golf on the course post tournament. Special parking or a special shirt only for committee chairs might mean more than a gift. Other perks that also build relationships are volunteer-only parties or early access to events. One organization that relied on volunteers to conduct fitness training quickly learned it was not a good idea to charge them for their materials. It is one thing to ask them to volunteer their time, but do not ask them to come out of pocket for costs. Sending them to conferences paid for by the organization has a double benefit, both to the organization as a result of the knowledge gained and to the individual who comes back motivated with newfound enthusiasm.

One benefit volunteers often cite is being in the know about the organization—having insider information. Volunteers enjoy spending time with staff and feeling part of the organization. Sharing the latest information and thinking with them before it becomes available to the general public is a motivating factor.

Logo wear has a dual benefit of promoting the organization and serving as a reward for the volunteers. It also serves to provide a sense of belonging among the volunteers.

Finally, recognition plaques or pins for years of service can increase retention. They become bragging rights in the office or at the organization's events. Sometimes accountability and recognition go hand in hand. Sharing participation levels such as number of volunteer hours among volunteers brings out the competitive nature and may improve engagement and outcomes. One organization bases promotion within the organization partially on the number of hours a volunteer works.

Overcoming Problems

Problem: Meetings drag on; action is rarely taken.

Solution: Provide committee data needed and a timed agenda with specific issues to be discussed and acted on in advance. Use a consent agenda for routine matters such as approval of minutes and acceptance of staff reports. Be realistic in what can be accomplished in one meeting. Keep discussion moving and control meeting so that while everyone has the opportunity to be heard, no one person controls the discussion. Require that everyone be recognized before speaking so they do not interrupt each other.

Problem: Lack of clear focus on committee's goals and responsibilities.

Solution: Provide written description of goals and responsibilities and reiterate it prior to each meeting. Ask the committee members to evaluate whether a particular task or activity is consistent with goals and responsibilities prior to moving forward with action on the task or activity.

Problem: Eighty percent of the work is done by 20% of the volunteers, while others lack commitment and do not participate or accept responsibilities.

Solution: When recruiting volunteers, ensure they understand their time commitment and responsibilities. Select enthusiastic, interested volunteers. At each meeting and online, provide a list of responsibilities and deadlines. As soon as volunteers begin exhibiting a lack of commitment, contact them and obtain feedback as to why they are not participating. Emphasize at each meeting the importance of not letting your fellow volunteers down by not participating.

Problem: Meetings are dominated by a few, some of whom have hidden agendas putting personal interests above those of the organization.

Solution: Instead of waiting for volunteers to speak, call on those whose views are not being heard. Require that attendees raise their hand and be recognized. Allow a set time period for volunteers to bring up their concerns.

Problem: Volunteers are unprepared for the meetings; they do not accomplish their assigned tasks in time for the meeting.

Solution: Ensure materials are available well in advance of the meeting. Ask volunteers to make a short presentation reporting what they have accomplished, and provide an outline of the presentation in advance of the meeting.

Problem: A volunteer is difficult to work with, has a negative attitude, and criticizes others, to the point no one wants to volunteer with them.

Solution: Chair can meet with the volunteer, giving them the opportunity to share concerns privately. Chair can use that opportunity to explain the impact their negative attitude is having on other volunteers. Chair can assign a duty that requires individual instead of group work. Chair can ask that they step off the committee unless behavior changes. If it is decided after counseling to terminate the volunteer, make sure all the issues and discussions are documented. Consult with legal counsel, and conduct the termination meeting in private but with more than one person present to document the meeting.

Problem: Committee members receive too much information and communication. They are starting to ignore important information because it is lost in volume of other information.

Solution: Ask staff to evaluate and prioritize information distributed. Consider having them provide bullet point updates and then target detail information to those who need that level of detail. Consider developing a dashboard of key indicators that shows progress.

Not letting volunteer management issues go on too long is the best way to effectively manage the volunteer team.

Reality Check

I will always remember a lesson my volunteer committee chairs taught me when I chaired a major festival that took a year to plan and involved thousands of volunteers. We were at critical juncture with lots of decisions required. I was all business pushing the group. I opened the meeting and jumped right into the business on the agenda. Then I looked up and everyone in the meeting had put on a clown nose. I got the message—we needed to remember to have fun.

The festival was a fun family–oriented event that was one of the most successful on the East Coast. It was easy to lose sight of the mission of what we were doing. We needed as a board to have fun and enjoy one another's company. It was up to the board leadership to lead by example. Sometimes you just have to laugh and have fun. The committee chairs were incredibly successful recruiters because they remembered what motivated the volunteers. Number one was to have fun—with one another—and to ensure an environment of good family fun was present at all times at the festival. Number two was they thanked their volunteers with both a kickoff and a post-event party (which was paid for by sponsors who recognized the importance of the volunteers in drawing attendees to the community). Each committee had its own volunteer golf shirt, so it was evident who was responsible for what and built connection among the committee members. Finally, volunteers were recognized for years of service by the mayor. Friendships were built and business was done, but the number one priority was safe fun from the board on down and especially at the festival events.

CHAPTER TWELVE

Thoughts on How a Board Member Becomes a Great Leader

The other chapters have discussed information needed by a board member to effectively serve a nonprofit organization. Therefore, by now you are technically capable of being a successful board member. However, leading your organization takes more than technical knowledge. It takes true leadership skills that are learned over time in leadership roles. Most are no different, whether you are leading a corporation, a country, or a nonprofit. These thoughts have been accumulated from various leadership books and from discussions with well-respected leaders. From the many sources these thoughts have been limited to the ones that, in the author's opinion, resonate most with situations that a nonprofit board member may face.

Take Care of Yourself

A leader needs to be able to handle stress and focus on leading the organization without other distractions. The first step is to focus on self-care. Think about what helps you to feel good. This includes eating properly, staying hydrated, getting sufficient sleep, exercising regularly, meeting your spiritual needs, and sometimes taking a break to do whatever you enjoy. Everyone hears about work–family balance, but in reality, it is better to think about four areas that are not "balanced" as in 25% of your time gets devoted to each but are integrated into each other, with priorities and focus changing each day. While the following representation (Figure 12.1) shows four similar sized shapes, they will vary in size each day.

Figure 12.1

Taking care of yourself has to come first, and some days may be a large component of your day. Priorities change with life changes. At certain points, your work career becomes a large circle as you, for example, start a new company or a new job or get a promotion. Other stages might be starting a family—with a new baby that family circle gets large. Community involvement may become a larger circle as you retire or on the day of a major event for your organization. By not putting pressure on yourself to balance all the circles, you can decide what your priorities are for that day and not feel guilty if that family circle shrinks. The concept of balance leads to self-criticism and trying to do everything equally well. It is just not possible every day.

Integrating your circles can also relieve stress and pressure. Bring your family to that charity event. Encourage your office workers to volunteer with you in the community.

Accept that the brain processes change as stress. Develop effective coping skills when you can't control every outcome and reaction. Losing control leads to a feeling of vulnerability and fear. However, trust overrides fear. Honoring the reaction you feel allows you to focus on challenging the conclusions and asking yourself what else might be true.

Consider how your behavior aligns with your values. You may want to do a values inventory. The website www.lifevaluesinventory.org is a good first step in helping you clarify your values and develop strategies for future development. Every great leader must have integrity, and integrity is exhibited by aligning your behavior with your values.

Self-care also means enjoying the present and celebrating small personal successes. In *Shakti Leadership* by Nilima Bhat and Raj Sisodia, ©2016 Berrett-Koehler Publishers, Inc., they point out that "you simply cannot be a conscious leader without being fully present. The leader not only has to look calm but actually be calm for their team and organization. Attaining that state of being takes effort and practice. . . . Presence is a state of relaxed concentration that can be cultivated." They go on to provide tools to achieve the calm state of present moment awareness.

Leaders Are Role Models

Think about the leaders you have admired and learned from. Are there specific characteristics that contributed to their success and resulted in you wanting to follow their example? Leaders must model the way. In earlier chapters we discussed board members being the first to contribute their time, talent, and treasure to the organization. That is modeling behavior. Never ask any volunteer to do something that you would not be willing to do. It sends a message when a leader is willing to take out the trash or serve meals or stay to help clean up after an event. Working side by side with all levels of stakeholders also gives the leader the opportunity to listen and observe what is going on. Some call this management by walking around. A new university president spent her first six months visiting every aspect of the institution and meeting with faculty, staff, alumni, donors, parents, and students. Some criticized her for not sharing her vision and plans for the university within the first couple months. By listening and observing, her vision was clearer, respectful of all stakeholders and well received. New board members should consider a similar listening period.

Speaking of role models, one president appears to stand out as a leader role model among all others—Abraham Lincoln. The book *Lincoln on Leadership, Executive Strategies for Tough Times* by Donald T. Phillips, published by Grand Central Publishing, ©2009 (*Lincoln on Leadership*), discusses his leadership strengths and how they allowed him to lead in the face of unprecedented adversity. The book points out that at his inauguration, "The country was divided, hatred was the most prevalent emotion, and there was no effective leadership anywhere in the government." And you think you have issues in your board role. As key leadership skills are addressed, those attributed to Lincoln will be described.

Lincoln was known for believing in management by walking around and his accessibility to the people. According to *Lincoln on Leadership*, Lincoln wrote to a general he was promoting about a general he was relieving of his command, " His cardinal mistake is that he isolates himself, and allows nobody to see him; and by which he does not know what is going on in the very matter he is dealing with." The book's author adds, "If subordinates, or people in general, know that they genuinely have easy access to their leader, they'll tend to view the leader in a more positive, trustworthy light." Being in regular contact with the stakeholders is a two-way street. Not only does the leader get to listen directly and not hear things thirdhand, but also it provides opportunity for teaching moments and for sharing the vision, mission, and values of the organization.

Another benefit of getting close to stakeholders is cultivating friendships and strong alliances. If they see you not only as the leader of the organization but also as a friend, they will be more likely to share concerns, be open to your point of view, and follow your lead. Leaders need to be friendly and amicable. There should never be a sense of superiority on the part of the leader. A great way to ensure they do not feel that way is to spend time with them on their "turf," such as in the staff's office or the volunteer's event site. Ask how you can help them do their job better. Ask what roadblocks they are facing and then try to remove them.

Integrity

A quote from a nominator of an individual for outstanding chief executive in the *Credit Union Management* magazine, November 2018, stated: "Joe naturally possesses the qualities required of great leaders: integrity, trust, passion, commitment, humility and empathy." The foundation of each of these qualities is integrity. Without integrity everything else collapses. It is what holds the organization together. A person with integrity is honest, upright, ethical, and moral. They have a high standard for always doing what is right, even when it may not be in line with the majority or popular opinion. Remember how we remember Abraham Lincoln as "Honest Abe." He exemplified integrity and honesty. As stated in *Lincoln on Leadership*, "Integrity must be sincere. That's one reason Lincoln was so admired in his lifetime. Through an individual's words, deeds, and actions, integrity can be judged to be genuine. And integrity is tied closely to the values espoused by an effective leader. As a rule, leaders must set and respond to fundamental goals and values that move their followers. . . . Put more simply, values motivate." It is the shared values that cause members to be passionate about the organization.

A leader with integrity takes fiduciary responsibility seriously, always putting the interests of the organization ahead of personal interests. A leader with integrity understands the policies, regulations, laws, and organizational documents and ensures compliance with them. A leader with integrity is fair to everyone and does not show bias. A leader with integrity does not have favorites who are given the best assignments. A leader with integrity can be trusted and builds that trust throughout the organization. Donors will only give to an organization led by leaders with integrity and who are trusted.

In his book *A Passion for Leadership*, Robert Gates emphasizes the importance of transparency in each of his roles from director of the CIA to president of Texas A&M University to secretary of defense. He states, "Ironically, the more information I was willing to share, the more people were inclined to trust me—and support what I was trying to do. I think that is almost always the case in leadership positions." Being open with your team, sharing both good news and bad news, builds trust and cooperation.

Passion and Commitment

As previously mentioned, board leadership is expected to devote their time, talent, and treasure to the organization. Why do they do it? They are passionate and committed to the organization. But there are levels of commitment and passion. Those board members who are just filling a seat, maybe show up half the time, and give a minimal donation lack passion and commitment. They will not inspire volunteers and will drag down the board. One cannot be a cheerleader for the organization if one is not passionate about the organization. Some may have a personal reason for being passionate about the organization, such as the mother of a Special Olympics athlete who went on to chair the board. Others may become passionate as they volunteer and see the good the organization does. Passion is contagious. Hearing leaders speak passionately and emotionally about the impact the organization has builds passion and commitment. Sometimes a video showing impact can spread passion. For example, one organization that supports an international eye hospital distributes a video showing how the lives of children and their families are changed once they receive treatment at the hospital. The leaders of the organization need to be able to articulate and demonstrate their passion. Ask each of your board members to write down why they want to serve on your particular organization's board. Ask them to describe what they see as the greatest impact the organization has on the communities they serve. In difficult times, it is passion and commitment that carry a leader through. The leader must be passionate about the mission of the organization or find another organization to serve.

Here is where the personality and presentation skills of a leader come into play. A leader may devote extensive time and effort to the organization and be passionate about the cause. However, if they cannot share that passion and exhibit that enthusiasm, they are not as strong a leader as your organization needs to inspire volunteers and donors. Sometimes coaching and training can move your leader to be more inspirational. Videotaping your leadership and playing it back while pointing out opportunities to build enthusiasm is helpful. When selecting your next chair, the nominating committee should consider the ability of each candidate to share their passion and commitment—not just behind the scenes but in front of all stakeholders. Too often a candidate is selected because they worked hard for the organization and served in every other role. Your board chair is often the face of the organization and needs to be able to enthusiastically share the passion and commitment to the cause.

Humility and Empathy

A great leader needs to relate well to the organization's volunteers, donors, staff, and beneficiaries. There is no room for a big ego. A great leader will not play the "I am chair" card or boast about how important they are. Being modest and humble helps a leader empathize with their constituency. A humble leader understands they are serving others versus others serving them. Understanding both your weaknesses and strengths forces the leader to be humble.

If you are humble, it is easier to understand the feelings of others and therefore empathize with them. Leaders who puts themselves in the shoes of another, whether it is another board member or someone receiving services from the organization, significantly increase the understanding of the other person's priorities, thought processes, and needs. The best negotiators are those who can empathize with the person they are negotiating with. And leaders often find themselves negotiating.

Empathy can best be built by interacting with others, another reason "management by walking around" is so important. As mentioned earlier, getting into the trenches with the team builds morale and also helps the leader empathize with those they lead. This also results in a cooperative team spirit. Teams want a leader they can look up to, but they also want to know that the leader understands them and "has their back." In addition to empathy, a leader must show support for the volunteers and staff. A leader must be prepared to go to battle for the team of staff and volunteers. If a criticism is levied against a member of the organization, it is the leader who should ensure the issue is investigated and, if found not to be warranted, the leader should strongly advocate for the team.

Listen, Listen, and Listen

Have you noticed that the less you talk and more you listen, the more information you gather? Poor leaders can develop egos and think they know all there is to know. They may try to force the group into making a decision they are not ready to make or only allow their own opinion to count. Ensuring that everyone has the opportunity to be heard results in more buy-in as the participants feel an integral part of the decision-making process. Those who listen attentively are perceived as better and smarter leaders. Show that you are listening by summarizing what you heard and asking questions to confirm your understanding. If a board chair does all the talking, they may be considered dictatorial and other board members may stop participating and disengage. Why should I speak, she is just going to do what she wants to do anyway?

Two-way listening builds relationships and then trust. As a leader, if you realize someone is diverting from the plan or attempts to circumvent the decisions of the leadership, it may be helpful to meet with that person and ask why. You may find by listening to each other that each realizes they have more in agreement than they thought. Asking the person to support your approach after listening to each other may be more palatable. Remember the old adage, "Keep your friends close and your enemies closer." Keeping those who disagree close provides insight into their point of view but only if you listen.

Leaders need to receive feedback but rarely ask for it. By accepting feedback about their performance, leaders are setting an example and demonstrate that they understand that they do not know it all and are committing to continuous learning and improvement. It demonstrates a certain vulnerability that can endear a leader to their team. Feedback from staff who often have a long history of working with board leadership over many years can be particularly helpful and further develops the relationship with staff. Feedback can also keep a leader from being "too confident" and keeps them grounded.

Direct reports and fellow board members may be hesitant to be honest, but if they understand that you honestly value their input, they may be open with their leader. They have to understand that you really do want to do better for the benefit of the organization they are passionate about. If they are still hesitant, you can offer for the feedback to be anonymous. However, a face-to-face meeting allows for the leader to ask follow-up questions or ask for clarification. Everyone benefits from the exchange of feedback, the leader, who learns where they can improve, and the staff or volunteer providing the feedback, who strengthens their trust in the organization and the leader.

Persuade, Direct, and Motivate

In *Lincoln on Leadership*, Lincoln states in remarks in the first Lincoln–Douglas debate in 1858, "He who molds public sentiment goes deeper than he who enacts statutes or pronounces decisions." Lincoln's oratorical skills were well known as a motivational factor in directing the military troops and building support among all his constituencies. With confidence and poise, present your decision or point of view supported by facts. Present them in a friendly manner, interjecting humor or entertaining stories if relevant. Sometimes it may seem more expeditious to dictate or force an action on the volunteers, but in the end getting everyone to understand and believe they were part of the decision-making is a better course to follow.

Sharing the vision and how the path to achieving that vision requires the decision or action also will motivate and persuade. Building passion around the vision and sharing confidence that the vision can be achieved are also important. Guiding your team to think big, while sharing how those big goals are achievable, one task at a time, will help move everyone in the same direction.

Having a winning attitude backed by even small successes or achievements will also motivate followers who want to be part of a winning team. Some leaders do not want to publicize their achievements. However, sharing the wins in a nonboastful manner (or having others do it for you), including thanking those who helped, makes the entire team feel like they have done well.

Another key characteristic that builds support is consistency. A leader cannot be constantly wavering or changing direction based on who was in front of them last. Sticking to the plan consistent with the vision is important. That does not mean that a leader should be inflexible. A leader needs to correct errors or change course as better information dictates. Again, communicating why a change was required is necessary. In a recent speaking engagement at the 2019 Credit Union National Association Government Affairs Conference, Alison Levine, the team captain of the first American Women's Everest Expedition, pointed out that sometimes you have to backup, regroup, and gather strength. "That is not the same as backing down." Hitting the pause button and changing course or going back to a previous point is necessary sometimes, and that is not failure. Situations change, and a great leader has to make decisions based on those situations. She related it to how her expedition of women was only 300 feet from the summit of Mt. Everest when a storm came up. As captain she had to make the tough decision to end the climb and head back down for the safety of everyone. That was not the plan, but the situation changed, so the plan had to change.

Leaders know that it is difficult to make decisions that result in significant changes in the organization. However, without a leader who is willing to be decisive and implement significant changes, an organization becomes stagnant and may lose both its supporters and volunteers. They miss opportunities. Staff are not motivated and become frustrated without challenges. You hear "We've always done it that way" as an excuse for being inefficient and ineffective. In the worst case, the organization may no longer be relevant and go out of existence. A leader fosters innovation and encourages continuous improvement.

A great leader doesn't allow subordinates to expect the leader to come up with all the solutions. Rather, a great leader encourages exploration of all the possible solutions prior to bringing a recommended path to the leader. A great leader sets an expectation with their volunteers that they will maintain their curiosity in order to develop their innovation skills. You have to build a culture of curiosity. The *Harvard Business Review* September 2018 article (https://hbr.org/magazine) "The Business Case for Curiosity" explains that curiosity is vital in helping organizations adapt to uncertain conditions and external pressures. This applies to nonprofit organizations as well as for-profit companies.

The previous chapter on strategic planning discusses the development of goals. A strong leader understands that it is the goals that keep the volunteers focused and moving forward in steps. Goals motivate and help focus efforts toward the vision. Often the vision may seem too far off in the future. The goals are more short term and can be attained within a year or so, creating a win for the team, again motivating the volunteers and keeping everyone on the same path forward.

How you treat your subordinates also impacts your ability to persuade and motivate. Referring to *Lincoln on Leadership*, "Lincoln essentially treated his subordinates as equals; they were colleagues in a joint effort. He had enough confidence in himself that he was not threatened by skillful generals or able cabinet officials. Rather than surround himself with 'yes' men, he associated with people who really knew their business, people from whom he could learn something, whether they were antagonistic or not." A strong leader looks for help from those who are more knowledgeable than they are. A strong leader also surrounds themselves with those whose skills complement the leader. If the leader is more technical, for example, a financial executive, they may want to find more creative, innovative board members. The leader also supports the subordinates, and particularly the staff, in success and failure. We often learn more from failures. The leader should monitor progress and prevent major failure but encourage the volunteers to try new approaches and be innovative. Again it is good to take calculated risks.

Respect and Recognition

A Passion for Leadership, Lessons on Change and Reform from Fifty Years of Public Service by Robert M. Gates, ©2016 Alfred A. Knopf publishers, emphasizes the importance of respect and recognition. He states, "For successful change at every kind of institution in both the private and the public sectors, a leader must win the support of those in the trenches who deliver the mission of the organization. Recognition of their critical role and respect for them go a long way." The previous chapter on volunteer engagement discusses formal recognition, but a great leader never misses an opportunity to recognize a team member with a thanks for a job well done. Often, just the fact the leader took the time to seek out the individual and point out how much their effort was appreciated means so much to the volunteer, staff member, or fellow board member. Looking for opportunities to recognize your team members in public allows them to be recognized in front of peers. If they deserve the recognition, give it to them often.

The personal contact with stakeholders helps the leader show appreciation for their efforts. Let them know the importance of their efforts in achieving the goals of the organization at every opportunity. A leader should empower their staff and volunteers and provide them with respect as well as opportunities for advancement. If they see their leader as their mentor who has confidence in them and shows they care for them, they will be more supportive. As Robert Gates states in *A Passion for Leadership*, they "will forgive a lot of the little mistakes that are inevitable."

Leaders understand that sometimes they will need to criticize those volunteers they lead. It is always best to do it in private with respect and a coaching approach. If a volunteer feels they have been harshly criticized, they will never volunteer or contribute again. Times can get tough, and when things go wrong, it gets tense. Take a deep breath, evaluate what should have been done differently, and then coach your team in private to prevent the situation from happening again.

A key to being a strong leader is to win the respect of those lowest in the organization. A leader needs to convince everyone they take their interests seriously. As Robert Gates stated in *A Passion for Leadership*, "Most new bosses—both in business and in the public sector—who want to change things don't make much of an effort to reach out to these folks." He went on to say, "The only way for a leader to persuade them he has their interests at heart is through consistent actions over a period of time. Rhetoric cuts no ice. But knowing the person at the top cares matters a lot, regardless of the kind of institution or its size." The more your volunteers see you and understand that you respect and value their efforts, the more they will support you and your plans.

Conflict

Leaders need to understand that conflict and disagreement can be productive. The leader though needs to be able to manage through conflict. The leader needs to see conflict as an opportunity for discovery. In February 2019, Robert Gates, former secretary of defense, commented in a discussion on civil discourse, "We have to learn to disagree without making it personal." You have to respect that a fellow volunteer or board member has a different point of view. He also pointed out that social media has made disagreement more public and that as differing points of view are more publicized it is harder to come together. Promotion of respectful disagreement is a tool of leadership. A leader should want to be surrounded by those who will disagree and point out if the leader is going down the wrong path. If you as a leader are surrounded by "yes" people, you won't know if you are going off course or the negative implications of a particular decision.

How can you as a leader encourage disagreement? Ask your team to tell you if they disagree. Let them know that you know you are not the smartest person in the room. Welcome criticism. Listen and incorporate what you hear into the discussion. Repeating the points of view indicates you have heard them. If a discussion becomes emotionally heated and therefore personal, the leader needs to call for a break. These disagreements should not become battles with winners and losers. Instead, all with differing points of view should learn from one another and possibly reach a compromise.

That does not mean that every decision and action gets diluted so that everyone is happy. Often adjusting planned action to build unanimous agreement keeps an organization from achieving all that it could, since a mediocre approach is agreed to. The organization becomes hesitant to take risks. It is important to take risks, but take calculated risks based on all available information. As Robert Gates points out in *A Passion for Leadership*, "A leader who seeks true reform will never get bold ideas or recommendations from task forces or working groups if consensus is the priority objective. Instead, a leader must instruct her task force chairs or subordinates leading other groups that consensus will only be valued if it represents agreement on something bold."

It is best to address conflict and disagreement face-to-face. Social media does not allow time for in-depth discussion and time to reflect. We all feel like we have to respond to that text or tweet immediately. Being able to look the person in the eye and establish a rapport with the person even while disagreeing facilitates respect for the other person's opinion. Face-to-face you can engage in humor and appear less threatening. It is easier to engage the other person in finding a mutually acceptable solution when you are in the same room. You can read your audience and understand the context of the point of view. As Robert Gates pointed out, "Capturing snapshots (as social media does) without context curtails the ability to mine the disagreement." He also pointed out the importance of engaging those who are facing the problem in the discussion and not just senior leadership.

As a leader, being willing to change your position after listening to all points of view is not a sign of weakness. Rather, it is a sign of an effective leader who acknowledges that others may have valid points of view and additional information that will result in the best possible outcome for the organization.

A leader also needs to know when it is time to move forward and get the board to come to a decision. There are times that a leader needs to call for a vote and abide by the results. Too many boards have leaders who allow a difficult decision to be tabled for further study until it just goes away, another lost opportunity for moving the organization forward. Once the disagreement is resolved and a decision or action plan is agreed to, the leader may need to rebuild relationships as the group comes together for implementation. Unfortunately, there may be those who decide they cannot continue in their roles and may resign from the board. It is best to accept their resignation, thank them for all they have done, and move the board forward. Remember you as the leader set the tone, so you must focus the board on the next steps and on the positive outcomes expected. As long as the decision process is open, fair, and transparent, the leader should be proud of the results of the disagreement—a clearer path forward.

Leading in a Crisis

When a crisis occurs, the board leader must be prepared to handle the situation. The primary leadership skill required is to remain calm—even if inside you feel panic. The leader must portray confidence, trust, and calm to lead his team. If the leader remains calm, it sets a tone for the entire organization to remain calm. Remaining calm allows the leader to think clearly as they make critical, often quick decisions. The entire team needs to know that the leader is engaged and involved in the entire response.

The leader should ensure there is a crisis or disaster recovery plan whether for a natural disaster or an accident involving injury to a participant/volunteer. The leader and the organization's executive director should plan ahead for the communication strategy. All communication to the public must be through one central person or representative such as a public relations firm experienced in handling crisis. Don't wait for a crisis to occur to hire that public relations firm because you won't have time to get them up to speed on your organization.

It is not enough to have drafted a crisis plan; leadership should ensure the plan is tested and communicated to all key leaders. A training session for leaders on what to do in a crisis can aid in feeling prepared to deal with a difficult situation. Everyone needs to come together, feel informed, and know the organization will get through the crisis.

It is during a time of crisis that a leader needs courage and confidence in themselves. The leader will face criticism, some of it unfair and inaccurate. Correcting the inaccuracies with honest truthful facts is the best way to address criticism. Ensure you have a complete understanding of what has happened and be transparent. Sometimes the leader has to be tough and believe that their decision, while not acceptable to everyone, was the right decision and move forward, ignoring the criticism. Never lose your composure or temper. Take a deep breath, pause, and maybe even write down what you would angrily like to say—but don't send it.

Reality Check

As you read this vignette, evaluate the leadership skills of the president of this alumni association. What are her strengths? What would you counsel her to do differently next time? Then ask yourself what your strengths and weaknesses are. Ask yourself how you want to be seen as a leader. Do a self-assessment against the key skills discussed in this chapter.

The president of the alumni association had just been elected by the board after serving as vice president. New to the organization was the executive director, hired six months prior. She had begun filling out her staff with new talent. A new vice president for university advancement had been in place for a year. One of his priorities was improving alumni engagement. He had an idea for a new engagement opportunity that had been a core engagement activity for more than 10 years at the institution he had previously served. It was an alumni weekend away from campus. He wanted the alumni association to implement a similar program.

One of the staff members had also come from that institution, and she knew exactly what needed to be done. The board was presented with the idea and identified a good initial location with many alumni. The new president was enthusiastic about the idea. She had her vision for the event. Her enthusiasm got the rest of the board excited, and the board voted to proceed with the event with an agreement to "invest" up to $25,000 (i.e., the weekend could lose up to $25,000) in the alumni weekend. Because the president had a background in finance, she wanted a budget developed immediately.

It was agreed to form a local planning committee of alumni active in the area. The planning committee included diverse demographics and backgrounds. At the initial meeting, the staff conducted the meeting. They handed out a listing of suggested events for the weekend that was patterned after the other university's established weekend. The president attended the planning meeting and quickly realized that her vision for the weekend was different than the staff's vision. She knew better than to debate the plans in front of the staff and planning committee. Instead, she redirected the discussion toward the planning committee and asked for their suggestions for potential activities and programs for the weekend. She listened for what they thought would be attractive to local alumni and attract alumni from around the country.

At her next regular meeting with the vice president of university advancement, the president expressed her concern about the vision for the weekend. They agreed to document a vision for the weekend to guide the team. By putting the thoughts down in writing, differences in approach were brought to light and could be discussed. The alumni association president wanted to think big. Her vision included a nationally known figure as a key speaker. And they had alumni who fit that bill. She forwarded the new vision to the board and held a board conference call to discuss. They agreed on the bolder vision and offered ideas on activities and speakers. They stepped forward offering sponsorship and a willingness to ask high-caliber, well-known personalities to speak.

One key figure agreed to be the keynote speaker, which added to the quality of the whole weekend. When asked about the format, he suggested that a national news commentator interview him. A quick check indicated a fee that was way above budget. The staff member, however, would not take "no" for an answer and e-mailed the commentator directly explaining the opportunity. The news commentator agreed. The alumni association president recognized the staff member and made sure that everyone, staff, board, and planning committee volunteers, knew what he had done just by not accepting "we can't afford that" as a "no."

The planning committee was kept informed, and quickly key volunteers emerged to ensure the entire weekend was a once-in-a-lifetime experience with special access to the best alumni leaders and venues the area had to offer. Enthusiasm spread and ideas became bolder. Since it was the first year, budgeting became a challenge and cost concerns grew. The president held regular meetings with staff and found herself questioning the costs of everything, from shipping costs to beverage costs—not the role of the president, which was pointed out to her when she solicited feedback.

The weekend was a great success thanks to the efforts of many. Volunteers were recognized and thanked. Staff were thanked both publicly at the event and privately, personally by the president after the event. She needed them to perform just as admirably next year when the weekend was held again in a different city. A tradition was started.

Index

Page numbers followed by *t* indicate tables.

About the Author

Cynthia Jarboe is consulting chief financial officer for the Emergency Assistance Foundation, a charitable foundation that aids corporations in providing emergency hardship grants to their employees. For the past 35 years, she has served on local, state, and national boards and as officer of dozens of nonprofits including the Virginia Special Olympics, as president of the William & Mary Alumni Association, as vice president of the Richmond YWCA, and as treasurer of the Society of International Business Fellows and the national fraternity Kappa Kappa Gamma. She is a former partner with Coopers & Lybrand, now PWC, the international accounting and consulting firm where she led its regional nonprofit audit practice. She has served as a speaker, consultant, and board advisor for several nonprofit organizations in the areas of best board practices, strategic planning, and financial sustainability.